IMAGES
of England

SHEFFIELD
CINEMAS

The Gaumont during the film week beginning Friday 28 June 1985. Opening as the Regent on Boxing Day 1927, this was Sheffield's first 'superkinema' with an atmosphere of opulence, which for many offered an escape from the drabness of ordinary life.

IMAGES
of England

SHEFFIELD
CINEMAS

Compiled by Clifford Shaw
for the Sheffield Cinema Society

TEMPUS

By the 1940s most of Sheffield's cinemas were advertising in *The Star*. A conspicuous absentee on VE Day, 8 May 1945, was the Victory Palace. The Abbeydale, Greystones and Page Hall cinemas were also hoping to attract some of the revellers to their ballrooms.

First published 2001, reprinted 2003

Tempus Publishing Limited
The Mill, Brimscombe Port,
Stroud, Gloucestershire, GL5 2QG

British Library Cataloguing in Publication Data.
A catalogue record for this book is available from the British Library.

ISBN 0 7524 2293 6

Typesetting and origination by Tempus Publishing Limited
Printed in Great Britain by Midway Colour Print, Wiltshire

Contents

Acknowledgements

Many of the photographs used in this book were derived from slides given to the Sheffield Cinema Society by Bernard Dore, its first President. However, they have been augmented from many sources, notably from the collections of Dave Richardson, John Wrigley, Kevin Wheelan and Martin Vickers; and from the photographic archive of Sheffield Local Studies Library. The Society is appreciative of the permission given by Sheffield Newspapers for the inclusion of a number of press photographs but our indebtness is far wider, for research into any aspect of local history is heavily dependent on the contemporary record provided by local newspapers.

From time to time photographs come to light. Sometimes they are preserved because of a family association. The album of photographs recording the exploitation of films shown at the Albert Hall was assembled by the showman himself, Reginald Rea. By chance they came into the possession of Andy Garner, a member of the Cinema Theatre Association, who kindly made them available. Credit is due to a number of other organizations or individuals who have provided photographs or given help in other ways. Inevitably some names will have been overlooked and a few have passed away, but for the record we offer our grateful thanks to Les Allen; Verna Archer; Stewart Bale; Beighton Historical Society; Peter Bolt; Stuart Brindley; C. Robin Brown; Frances Buckley; Ray Byers; Chapeltown and High Green Archive; Frank Coupe; Allen Eyles; Peter England; Peter Fletcher; Mrs D.M. Hunt; Ron Hanlon (Odeon Ltd); Greta Hanson; Harrison Cameras of London Road, Sheffield; Leslie Johnson; Steve Kay; Colin Kirkham; Ron Moss; John Potter; Henry Priestley; Constance Pullen; Brian Roe; Cyril Slinn; Rosemary Sloane; Stuart Smith; Bill Stephenson; Mrs Tillbrook; the University of Sheffield Union of Students and Film Unit; Ian Walker; Andrew Woodhead; H. Alvery Wadsworth and Dorothy Ward.

Richard Ward's *In Memory of Sheffield's Cinemas* was published in 1988 and set a high standard but there is always more to learn. My research has been undertaken mainly at the National Newspaper Library, Colindale, the library of Sheffield Hallam University and, not least, the City Central Libraries and Archives. The Society would wish to thank Doug Hindmarch and his staff in the Local Studies Library and, in particular, Mike Spick for providing copies of prints held in the photographic collection.

Introduction

Sheffield's first cinema was the Central Hall, Norfolk Street, which was opened by Jasper Redfern on 10 July 1905, but the films were always accompanied by variety acts. Previously, animated pictures had been included in variety programmes at the Sheffield Empire from June 1896 and shortly afterwards at the Grand Theatre, West Bar, and the Alhambra, soon to be renamed the Attercliffe Palace; films were also shown at the Albert Hall, the Montgomery Hall and Sheffield's fairgrounds. The Theatre Royal, Attercliffe, had turned to pictures in the summer of 1906 and from February 1907 they were shown on a regular basis; the Grand Theatre followed in December 1908 and the Attercliffe Palace in June 1909. However, both Attercliffe halls showed some turns and by 1920 the palace was again a variety theatre.

The Sheffield Picture Palace in Union Street was the first hall to be designed as a cinema and opened in August 1910. The second was the Electra, which opened in February 1911 and had been commissioned by Sheffield and District Cinematograph Theatres. The company was also responsible for building the Cinema House in 1913 and the Carlton in 1938, having in the intervening years taken control of the Globe in 1919 and the Don in 1927. A second local circuit was established by Elisha C. Clayton, who in 1920 launched Heeley and Amalgamated Cinemas, a company that brought together the Heeley Palace, the Woodseats Palace, the Oxford Picture Palace and the Pavilion, Attercliffe. In 1921 Hallamshire Cinemas established a third local circuit, comprising the Crookes, Darnall and Weston Picture Palaces; a close association also developed with the Lansdowne Picture Palace and the Sunbeam.

Between 1910 and the onset of the First World War in August 1914, thirty cinemas had been completed or were in the process of being built. In 1918 the Albert Hall came into regular use as a cinema. A further twelve cinemas were opened between 1920 and 1922, although the construction of some had been delayed due to the priority given to house building. No further cinemas were built until 1927, when the Manor Cinema and the Regent, Barker's Pool, were opened within a fortnight. The Regent and Albert Hall were soon to be controlled by Gaumont British, while in 1931 ABC leased the Hippodrome, a 1907 variety theatre, for use as a cinema. In the mid-thirties the Salford-based J.F. Emery circuit acquired the Star, the Wicker and also the Regal, which was a recently completed replacement for the Theatre Royal, Attercliffe. Between 1934 and September 1939 seven cinemas were constructed that were intended to cater for the developing housing estates. Of these, the Forum and Capitol were commissioned and managed by Michael J. Gleeson, the building contractor, who also owned the Ecclesfield Cinema House. The three cinemas were sold to Essoldo late in 1947 but were not renamed Essoldo until 1950 or, in the case of the Forum, 1956. Sheffield's first Odeon was started in 1939 but due to the onset of war never got beyond the girder stage. The Odeon chain had emerged during the 1930s as a major circuit but, following the death of Oscar Deutsch in 1942, it operated alongside Gaumont British within the Rank Organization. Star Cinemas was by comparison a small part player but the company gained control of the Palace, Stocksbridge, in 1942; the Lyric, Darnall, in 1943; and the Palace, Chapeltown, in 1944. There were no further acquisitions in Sheffield until 1955 when Star Cinemas took over the seven halls in the Heeley and Amalgamated and J.F. Emery circuits. To these would later be added the Manor Cinema, the Hillsborough Park, the Ritz and Cinecenta.

After the war no new cinemas were built in Sheffield until the Odeon, Flat Street, in 1956 and the ABC in 1961. Cinecenta with two small auditoria and Cineplex with three opened respectively in 1969 and 1972. The Regent (the Gaumont since 1946) was 'twinned' in 1968/69 but surprisingly closed in 1985; the Odeon, Burgess Street, a smaller cinema, was included in a development on the site but did not open until 1987. Sheffield's first multiplex was the AMC at Crystal Peaks with ten screens but it was soon to become part of the UCI circuit. In 1992 Odeon 7 opened with seven screens; it was a reconstruction within the shell of the former Fiesta night club but included the Cinecenta auditoria. Warner Cinemas at Meadowhall followed in 1993 with eleven screens. The Showroom cinema occupied part of a converted building and opened in 1995 with two screens; with the aid of a lottery grant two further auditoria were added in 1998. The Virgin (now UGC) eclipsed all other Sheffield cinemas when it opened in November 1998 with twenty screens.

In the period between the outbreak of war in September 1939 and the Blitz in December 1940 there were fifty-three cinemas in Sheffield with a seating capacity of around 56,300. Four Sheffield cinemas did not reopen following war damage, while the Scala was forced to close in 1952 as a result of steps taken by Sheffield University to expand teaching facilities. From 1957, cinema closures became widespread because of dwindling audiences. The last surviving suburban cinemas were the Abbeydale and the Vogue (originally the Capitol), both of which closed in 1975, and the Rex, which hung on until 1982. The Odeon, Flat Street had been dedicated to bingo since 1971. The Electra (the News Theatre from 1945 and then the Classic from 1962) closed in 1982, while the Wicker (as studios 5, 6 and 7) finally closed in 1987. The ABC (now Cannon) closed in 1988 and the Cineplex (the Anvil from 1983) in 1990. The short lived Odeon, Burgess Street, closed in 1994 in anticipation of an extension to Odeon 7.

In 2001 there are only five cinemas in Sheffield but fifty-five auditoria. The total seating capacity of 11,826 is substantial but only about one fifth of the peak figure in 1940. On the other hand it is an encouraging increase on the 1984 level of 4,034, when both the Gaumont and the ABC were still open. In retrospect 1984 is seen as the year when nationwide cinema attendances were at their lowest ebb, but since then attendances have been edging up most years. Even for those who nowadays go little, if at all, to the cinema there is a degree of pleasure in thinking back over highlights from the past. So let's go to the pictures, even if it only involves settling back turning the pages.

One
Yesterday's Leading Picture Houses

For a time during the 1920s Reginald Rea, the manager of the Albert Hall, placed his press advertisements under the heading 'Sheffield's leading picture house'. The name of the cinema was not even mentioned. The Sheffield Picture Palace and the Central Picture House could have made the claim with equal, and possibly greater, justification, while the Cinema House was also up with the leaders. These were the 'first run' cinemas, a privilege bestowed by the renters in return for the higher revenue earned from such bookings. Later 'first run' cinemas were the Regent (from 1927) and the Hippodrome (from 1931). This meant that these cinemas had first refusal of films in distribution and, if they chose to exercise it, other cinemas were 'barred' and must wait. The Albert Hall was destroyed by fire in 1937, while the Central did not reopen following Blitz damage in 1940. After the war the Odeon, Flat Street (from 1956) and the ABC (from 1961) claimed their place in the sun. By the 1980s the circumstances had changed greatly and the 'barring' system was outlawed in the Cinemas Act, 1985. The Odeon, Burgess Street, which opened in 1987, had only two screens and was the last of Sheffield's old-style cinemas.

A point of detail needs to be made, which is generally applicable. Seating capacities are quoted around the time a hall opened or came into use as a cinema. These figures have not been revised unless there was a major reconstruction such as the installation of a balcony or the extension or division of an auditorium. The general trend was of falling capacities as seating was re-spaced to provide greater comfort and more leg room. In cinemas built before the First World War seating in the cheapest parts of the house was often of a bench type. Even where individual tip-up seats were provided throughout, there is likely to have been an appreciable reduction in capacity over the life of the cinema.

The Gaumont in August 1946, only a few weeks after the Regent had been renamed; the Cinema House is on the left.

The Sheffield Picture Palace, Union Street, in July 1961 when the feature was *The Rat Race*. The exterior was in a modified renaissance style and surfaced in white faience, a form of glazed terracotta. It had opened on 1 August 1910. The capacity including balcony seating was 1,000. Newton Chambers occupied adjacent property and supplied the hot water used in heating the cinema from their own boilers; it was many years before an independent water supply was available. Apart from a period during and immediately after the First World War, Len Shaw was manager from the time the cinema opened until 1954, when he suffered a stroke. Shaw used to make 'topicals' of events of local interest and would even show them at the palace on the same evening. Undoubtedly he was a live wire and innovator with strong and sometimes unorthodox personal views. The hall never opened on Good Friday and rarely on Christmas Day – often it was the only cinema in Sheffield not to do so. It refrained from showing advertising films and for a time did not even show trailers to publicize coming attractions. The Palace would often close for one or two weeks at the end of July; this enabled many of the staff to take their holidays at a time when business was slack and also provided an opportunity to carry out scheduled redecoration or improvements. Although there was a stage and six dressing rooms, these were rarely used except for a period in 1929, when cine-variety was given an extended trial in a vain attempt to boost the fading charms of the silent cinema. Around this time *The Jazz Singer* was shown but in a silent version; music was provided by an augmented orchestra, while Dennis Allison, a popular vocalist, sang all the Jolson numbers. In the mid-1950s the advent of Cinemascope was well exploited, the Palace being the main city centre cinema to show films in Scope with the enhancement of stereophonic sound, which at that time was recorded on a magnetic track. The Palace closed on 31 October 1964.

The Cinema House, Barker's Pool, 1913. This was also faced with white faience, highlighted by a magnificent tower. An imposing feature of the building was a grand staircase leading to a balcony foyer, which was also used as a tea room. Seating capacity was about 800. The Cinema opened on 6 May 1913 and in the early months showed a series of shorts in Chronochrome, an early colour process. Chronochrome negatives provided red, green and blue colour records, each occurring every third frame. A special projector was necessary, moving the film three frames at a time and operating at 48 frames a second, which was about three times the normal speed. An out-of-the-ordinary event was a visit by the King of Uganda, when he attended an illustrated talk on bees. In 1914 talking shorts were including in programmes for some ten weeks, using an early sound system that depended on disc recordings. By 1920 'The Cinema', as it was sometimes referred to, was floodlit and displayed an illuminated sign. The Cinema House was more likely than other Sheffield cinemas to show occasional nature films, for example, Flaherty's Nanook of the North, which was shown for two weeks in 1922 and – with a soundtrack – 1949. Often programmes included musical interludes, the orchestra eventually performing on a raised dais; the pieces to be played were sometimes included in press advertisements. In 1923 'wireless apparatus' was installed and selected transmissions were relayed to the audience. Another innovation was a machine that dispensed programmes giving 'coming attractions'; a few of them bore a lucky number and, if retained until the end of the month, when the winning numbers were disclosed, the holder could claim a prize. The proprietors were more cautious than many in deciding that sound had come to stay. The first sound film was shown at the end of February 1930; it was Climbing the Golden Stairs, a short in Technicolor.

The Cinema House, February/March 1939. The sound system had recently been upgraded by the installation of the latest BTH equipment. *Pygmalion*, starring Leslie Howard and Wendy Hiller, enjoyed a run of four weeks, which at the time was quite exceptional. It played for a further week at the end of August.

The Cinema House, December 1960. By now the cinema was mainly playing double bills of features that had previously been released. A larger screen had been installed in 1953 but *The Conqueror* and other films in Cinemascope were not seen to advantage, most probably because the position of the balcony limited the size of the image that could be projected.

The Cinema House, October 1961. The cinema had been sold to property developers in 1959 but did not close until '12 August 1961. The last programme of *The Horse Soldiers* and *The Devil's Disciple* is still showing on one of the bills.

The Cinema House, Christmas Eve 1961. While demolition is well under way, the proscenium arch and screen are still in position. Somewhat unusually, the screen was at the same end of the hall as the entrance.

The Central Picture House, February/March 1922. The film that is being shown is the silent version of *Disraeli* made in 1921. The Central had opened on 30 January 1922. The frontage on the Moor was restricted but the auditorium was quite large, seating 600 in the balcony and 1,000 downstairs; there were tip-up seats throughout. Waiting space for 500 was provided inside the building. There was a ground-floor smoking room and lounge, a café-restaurant on the second floor and a large billiards room on the lower floor. The opening programme included Doris Keane in *Romance*, a film of the Prince of Wales in India and *The Children's Home* accompanied by the singing of Ida Bloor. The orchestra initially played from the balcony but this practice was soon discarded. Quite often there were special presentations in which vocalists were supported by an augmented orchestra. In 1926 a three-manual cinema organ was installed, built by Vincent and Sewell of Sunderland; Arnold Bagshaw, the musical director, became resident organist and remained until the early thirties. In 1929 the Central Picture House took over the Sunday services previously held at the Albert Hall – however, they were discontinued in 1935. Various improvements were carried out in the 1930s, the main structural work being undertaken in 1935; this aimed at improving the frontage and providing a wider entrance hall. In 1937 the Central became the first Sheffield cinema to install Western Electric's latest sound system for which the term 'mirrophonic' was coined. In January 1939 Anna Neagle and producer Herbert Wilcox made a personal appearance to publicize *Sixty Glorious Years*, a successor to *Victoria the Great*. During the war the Central was the only Sheffield cinema that was prepared to open on a Sunday under a scheme in which admission would have been mainly restricted to those serving in the Forces. It proved to be for one performance only, which was on 7 December 1940, for the Blitz followed five days later. Len Sullivan, the manager, was on duty and, when fires broke out, he shepherded those who had stayed to neighbouring shelters. That was the Central's last picture show.

The Central Picture House, July/August 1929. It was a dead heat. The Central and the Regent both installed Western Electric sound equipment and were showing 'talkies' from Monday 17 June 1929. Al Jolson's *The Singing Fool* at the Central proved very popular and was followed by the even more successful *The Broadway Melody*.

The Central Picture House undergoing demolition, May 1961. Considerable damage had been caused by incendiary bombs but the building was not beyond repair. A possible restoration after the war was frustrated by the restrictive conditions imposed by the planning authority, which was intent on a comprehensive redevelopment of the Moor.

The Albert Hall, October 1928. The scene looks alarmingly real but it was all a publicity stunt. Those were the days. The Albert Hall opened as a concert hall on 15 December 1873 with a main entrance on Barker's Pool. The great hall was on the first floor; along three sides there was a balcony but at the back was a second balcony tier and an upper gallery. There was an organ, which was an exceptionally fine instrument built in Paris by Monsieur Cavaille-Col. Among the musical events that emerged were a series of Saturday night popular concerts, which sometimes included variety artists, 'animated pictures' being first shown in September 1896. Over the years many showmen came to the Albert Hall with programmes of short films, often mixed in with other forms of entertainment: many of the bookings ran for one night only but varying periods of up to three weeks were not uncommon. In December 1912 the main hall was leased to a small Leeds firm which intended to run it as a cinema, but the enterprise was not a financial success and the trial period of twelve months was not extended. During the First World War the hall was used for showing films on an occasional basis and in December 1917 *Intolerance* was given its Sheffield première. Films were shown more regularly in the following year and from 17 June 1918 the Albert Hall operated as a normal cinema. Once it became clear that its full-time use as a cinema had given the Albert Hall a new lease of life, extensive work was carried out. Starting in May 1919, this occupied a period of sixteen months, although the cinema remained open. A proscenium was constructed and new curtains fitted to narrow the wide expanse of the stage; a new operating booth was built and the projectors were replaced. In 1924 coloured 'rocket lights' designed to catch the eye were installed on the top of the cinema, while the basement was converted to provide covered waiting space. In June 1927 the cinema closed for six weeks; extensive alterations included remodelling of the foyer and the erection of a canopy along the entire front and side of the building. Seating capacity was probably a little over 1,600. Reginald Rea, who was manager at the Albert Hall from 1919 to 1929, had an undoubted flair for catching the public's eye, but his stunt to promote *Fire* was surely tempting fate. A real fire on 14 July 1937 resulted in the building being destroyed.

The auditorium of the Albert Hall, probably after the cinema had reopened in July 1927. The proscenium had been reconstructed to increase the depth of a shallow stage, while the hall had been entirely refurnished and redecorated. The Holophane lighting system had been installed; this could provide a variety of lighting effects including a prismatic colouring of the screen curtains. The organ is hidden from view; the organist could only see the screen or musical director through a system of mirrors.

Weston Park in May 1926 provided the setting for a publicity shot designed to promote both the Albert Hall and *The Eagle* (watch my feet!). *The Eagle* starred Rudolph Valentino.

The Albert Hall foyer in March/April 1925, transformed to publicize a fortnight's run of Douglas Fairbank's fantasy, *The Thief of Bagdad*. A number of staff members are in costume.

Reginald Rea's most famous exploit was in July 1928, when he was photographed from the air, standing on the wing of a plane in flight. This was intended to focus attention on the British naval film *Carry On*, which was a coming attraction at the Albert Hall. Rea wisely did not attempt to repeat the experience and finally retired from a post as cinema manager at Newport in the Isle of Wight at the age of eighty-one.

Barker's Pool, May 1928. The Albert Hall and the Regent represent the old and the new. *Dawn* at the Albert Hall was a story about the nurse Edith Cavell, who was shot as a spy during the First World War. The Regent had opened on Boxing Day, 1927. The big picture evidently starred Wallace Beery.

The café-restaurant at the Regent was at a mezzanine level and decorated in a Georgian style with panelled walls and an ornate ceiling; it was not restricted to cinema patrons and could seat about 150.

The upper part of the Regent auditorium, *c.* 1928. Sheffield's first 'superkinema' was in the Italian Renaissance style. A white faience facing enclosed a recessed entrance and formed a broad plinth along the base of the frontage; there was a separate entrance to the front stalls from Burgess Street. Colour was freely used throughout the auditorium and there was a wealth of rich detail – ornamental ceiling motifs, fluted pilasters and decorated panels. Seating capacity was 2,300, which included 850 in the circle. A feature of the large auditorium was a huge double dome and beautifully proportioned proscenium arch. The dome was constructed with an open grille outside and easily operated roller shutters; the effect achieved was similar to a sliding roof. The console of the Wurlitzer organ operated on a lift, enabling the organist to perform in full view of the audience. The organ loft was built onto the roof, the sound entering the auditorium through a grille running the whole length of the proscenium arch. The stage was well equipped and was 27ft deep; there were seven dressing rooms. The golden age of cine-variety at the Regent was during the eighteen-month period between its opening and the coming of sound. Some of the more familiar names that appeared were Will Hay, Teddy Brown, Mr Flotsam and Mr Jetsam and the Houston sisters.

Projection was from the lower part of the dome. The operator could only reach the projection booth by ascending a spiral staircase from the rear circle, then going into the open and across the roof, and finally down another set of steps. Twenty-six years later, the management was faced with a problem in the run-up to Cinemascope. The angle of projection was too great to obtain a sharp picture over the whole of the greatly enlarged screen and it was found necessary to reposition the projection booth at the back of the circle.

Below opposite: The Gaumont, December 1949. The attractive display is clearly designed to evoke a charitable thought for the less fortunate. The week's film was Danny Kaye in *The Inspector General*; *Mr Ace* with George Raft was showing on Sunday only.

Above: The Gaumont auditorium, 1965. A large, curved screen had been installed in readiness for the coming of Cinemascope in February 1954 but it was fixed and needed to be replaced by a movable screen to enable the stage to be brought back into use for live shows. This work and other improvements were carried out in 1959, including the construction of a new orchestral pit; the auditorium was entirely redecorated. The cinema closed for ten days in August 1962 after a storm had found a weakness in the flat roof. Despite costly remedial work there was a fall of fibrous plaster some two years later, which was probably a result of previous damage. Stage presentations in the sixties were one night stands and not accompanied by films. Among the artists who appeared were Cliff Richard, Eddie Cochran, Bobby Darin, Victor Borge, Nina and Frederick, the Rolling Stones, the Beatles and Count Basie and his orchestra.

The Gaumont in May 1960, when the feature was *Never so Few* with Frank Sinatra as a combatant in the Burma jungle. The café is now described as the Green Room restaurant, possibly as a result of the introduction of potted plants. In 1966 it was remodelled, creating a more contemporary style, and illuminated panels carried various hallmark motifs. The restaurant was reduced in size following 'twinning' in 1969, while ten years later it was sacrificed in the creation of Gaumont 3.

The Gaumont, April 1965. The long queue was for *Mary Poppins* with Julie Andrews. *The Intelligence Men*, in which Morecambe and Wise made their film début, is showing at the Odeon.

Gaumont 1 auditorium in 1969, showing the Cinerama screen which was 70ft wide. In October 1968 the Gaumont closed for over nine months while the roof was raised some 15ft and the interior reconstructed to provide twin auditoria. Gaumont 1 was on the upper floor and seated 737.

Gaumont 2, 1969. Gaumont 2 was the larger auditorium on the ground floor and seated 1,150; both auditoria were capable of screening 70mm prints. New projectors had been installed; lens and aperture plates could be changed automatically via the 'Cinemation' unit. Gaumont 2 also eventually benefited from the introduction of 'cakestands' so that spools were only used occasionally; Gaumont 1 continued to run on spools.

In Gaumont 1 the rear portion of the auditorium is quite steeply tiered, the aisles being stepped; the basic colour scheme was sea green. Gaumont 1 was reached through a tunnel stairway rising from the right of the main foyer to the upper lounge.

A view of Gaumont 2 with a chance to see the screen curtains, which were once regarded as the *sine qua non* of screen presentation. The basic colour scheme in the auditorium was bright red. The screen size was 25ft by 19ft for the normal 'wide screen' ratio, or 44ft by 19ft for Cinemascope.

The entrance to Gaumont 3 with Eunice and Dorothy. In those days the spotlight was turned on the girl with the tray standing at the front of the auditorium. Selling ice-cream was quite an art.

Gaumont 3 opened in December 1979 and was referred to as the 'mini', as it had only 144 seats. The necessary space had been created by utilizing the bar, restaurant and kitchen area; it had not involved closure of the principal auditoria. It was never equipped for Dolby stereo-sound. Gaumont 3 was mainly used as a third port of call for films nearing the end of a successful run.

The Gaumont, June/July 1985. During 'twinning' the original Regent façade was largely preserved but it had been redecorated in primrose 'Sandex'. The entrance was faced with unglazed ceramic tiles, while publicity frames were of burnished aluminium. Fortified by the major refurbishment in 1968/69, the cinema appeared to be a firmly entrenched part of the Barker's Pool scene; but it was not to be.

The Gaumont entrance foyer looks quite lived-in. Ice-cream and drinks cartons are being put to good use; in the background is a video shop.

The Gaumont, September 1985. The circuit management felt that the Gaumont was an expensive cinema to run and was mindful of the fact that audiences appeared still to be shrinking. Negotiations had been entered into with a potential developer on the basis of accepting a lease that would enable Rank Theatres to maintain a presence in Sheffield city centre but in smaller auditoria. *Desperately Seeking Susan* was still showing when the Gaumont closed on 7 November 1985.

Gaumont 1 again. A tier of fifty-six Pullman seats was installed in 1971. These were the height of luxury for they were individual armchairs with quilted cushions.

Paul Archer came as general manager to the Sheffield Gaumont in 1971 on the retirement of Roy Raistrick. Here he is pictured with David Puttnam and Sir Richard Attenborough during British Film Year in 1985. This was an attempt to promote cinema-going in Britain. A circus-style exhibition toured the country, reaching Sheffield in September, where a tent was erected on the Fargate precinct. Robert Powell was the celebrity appearance, while Paul Archer, Les Allen and other local cinema managers met members of the public.

Paul and Verna in the company of Michael Palin at the formal opening of Odeon 7 in March 1992.

The Gaumont was demolished in 1986, a sad ending for a magnificent cinema. However, on this occasion there was promise of a Phoenix to arise from the rubble.

Sheffield's first pre-war Odeon never got beyond the girder stage. The Odeon, Burgess Street, is doing rather better but it proved to be short lived, although providing excellent viewing conditions while it was still open.

The Odeon, Burgess Street, February 1994. The building proved to be of an unusual and controversial design. The façade of mirrored glass reflecting the sky and surrounding buildings is not unattractive but the obtrusive steel framework painted a garish red has found few admirers. The cinema opened on 20 August 1987. The entrance from Burgess Street was undistinguished but, once past the rather cramped vestibule, the way ahead to the auditoria was up a handsome stairway. About halfway up, this divided and passed on each side of a panoramic mural to reach a landing at parterre level. A short flight of steps led to the first floor, Odeon 1 being along a corridor on the left; Odeon 2 was on the right and accessed up a further short stairway. Odeon 1 seated 500 and the capacity of Odeon 2 was 324; both offered a high standard of comfort and an uninterrupted view of the screen. Odeon 7 had opened in March 1992 and the management was conscious of the additional costs in operating from two sites. The opportunity arose of providing three additional auditoria in the multi-storey development off Arundel Gate through leasing space vacated by previous tenants. Although negotiations had not then been finalized, the Odeon, Burgess Street, closed on 20 February 1994.

A section of an extensive mural, best seen from above on leaving after a performance. It was painted by Joe Scarborough, assisted by Bill Kirby, and depicted some of the entertainments that have been part of the Sheffield scene. It did not prove possible to preserve the mural in the conversion of the building for use as a nightclub.

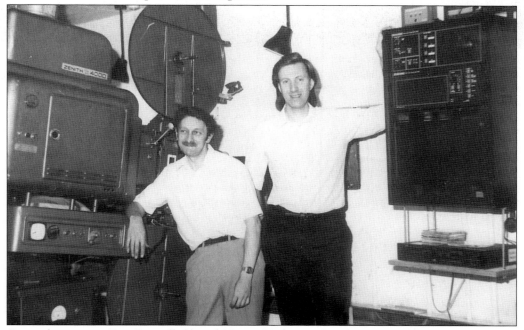

Comrades in arms: Ray Byers (left) and Martin Vickers in booth two. Ray Byers was appointed Chief Projectionist, having come from Bolton. Martin Vickers was Senior Projectionist, having worked at the Gaumont from 1969 and previously at the Classic. The projector was a Cinemeccanica Victoria 8, lit by Zenith X40 xenon lamps.

The Odeon, Flat Street, still showing the programme that opened the cinema on 16 July 1956. Construction of Sheffield's first Odeon started in 1939 but was suspended on the outbreak of war. The post-war cinema had been redesigned and was mainly of rustic brick. An unusual feature was a glass-walled, wedge-shaped entrance foyer, which projected forward at half height from the main building. A large advertising display covered the whole of the foyer apex well above the entrance and canopy. The auditorium was unusually wide and a continuous cove linked walls and ceiling. Of the 2,340 seats, 816 were in the circle. The Odeon took many of the spectacular large-screen epics, which were 'roadshown' at higher than usual prices. Films shown in Todd-AO included *South Pacific*, *Cleopatra* and notably *The Sound of Music*, which ran for sixteen months. After the 'twinning' of the Gaumont in July 1969, the roles of the two cinemas were reversed and the Odeon took a greater number of ordinary releases. Somewhat surprisingly the Odeon closed on 5 June 1971. Three months later it reopened as the Top Rank Club (now Mecca) and for the past thirty years has remained a popular venue for bingo.

The Odeon, Flat Street, as a Top Rank bingo club, *c.* 1989.

The Hippodrome, October 1955, when the film showing was *The Prodigal*. The Hippodrome had opened as a music hall in 1907 and was the work of the well-known theatrical architect Bertie Crewe. The frontage to Cambridge Street was in terracotta with granite pillars and marble enrichments. Over the central portico the name of the theatre was surrounded by designs symbolic of art, music and drama. Although many famous names were to appear at the hall, it was never quite as successful as the Empire. In 1931 it was leased to Associated British Cinemas, who carried out a number of structural alterations, including the construction of a new projection booth at the back of the circle. The Hippodrome reopened as a cinema on 20 July with a seating capacity of around 2,450. An unusual feature of the building was the sliding roof, which continued to be used in hot weather during its years as a cinema. In 1938 it closed for three weeks, various improvements being carried out including reseating and redecoration. Sunday opening was not allowed in Sheffield until August 1944. Sunday programmes at the Hippodrome differed from those shown during the rest of the week and this remained the usual practice, even when the other city centre cinemas were playing the same programme for the full seven days. In 1948 the company that had previously run the Tivoli raised additional capital to buy the Hippodrome and moved in when ABC hesitated over securing a new lease. In 1953 the Hippodrome became the place to see 3D with such films as *House of Wax*, *Hondo* and *Kiss Me Kate*. The process involved twin cameras recording two view points, which were then projected and superimposed on the screen; the audience wore special glasses which, although colourless, polarized light on different planes. In 1954 a larger panoramic screen was installed, the first film in Cinemascope being shown in October. Since it had been a cinema no attempt had previously been made to use the stage but in May 1956 a series of plays were presented that were sponsored by the Moral Rearmament movement; a distinguished member of the company was Reginald Owen, an English character actor who had appeared in many pictures at MGM. The gallery was taken out of use in December 1959; 913 seats were still available in the stalls and 506 in the circle.

The Hippodrome in the final week, when the feature was *Gone with the Wind*, a film that had previously played at the Hippodrome in 1942, 1944, 1948, 1952 and 1962. The cinema had been under the threat of demolition since 1960 in consequence of a redevelopment scheme and its fate was sealed when it was sold to property developers. It closed to a full house on 2 March 1963.

The ABC, Angel Street, May-August 1975, when *The Towering Inferno* was showing in 70mm. It was constructed of pre-cast concrete columns with brick in-fill panels and faced with Portland stone. Prominent features were a large window frame with green slates which highlighted the refreshment lounge; and a canopy over the entrance with a brilliantly lit soffit.

The main ABC auditorium as it appeared around the time when the cinema opened on 18 May 1961. From the entrance foyer and paybox it was approached up a wide staircase, which led to an upper foyer and refreshment lounge, which was on two levels. To the left on the lower level was a passage leading to a vestibule and entrance fairly close to the front of the house. Further along the upper level was an entrance to the back of the auditorium, where seats were originally more expensive. The auditorium seated 1,327 and was of a stadium type: instead of a traditional proscenium there was a vast curtain that continued along the side walls. There was a floating ceiling in midnight blue, dotted with star lights and simulating a night sky, although at the back of the house a change in ceiling interest was introduced. The size and shape of the screen was adjustable and could cope with up to five picture formats; the width of the screen was 60ft, which in 1961 was possibly the largest in Britain. The sound installation was able to reproduce both optical and magnetic tracks. In 1975 the refreshment lounge was converted into ABC 2, a small auditorium seating only 94. The first film in Dolby stereo sound was not until December 1978, the installation being restricted to the main auditorium. Throughout the 1960s and 1970s Albert Brierley was based at the Sheffield ABC but toured with a Hammond organ round other cinemas in the circuit.

Les Allen, the manager of the Sheffield ABC from 1969 to 1986. The lamphouses used in association with Philips DP 75 projectors were particularly suitable for 70mm screenings as the gates could be water-cooled so that the intensity of the arcs could be increased to add brightness to the screen.

The Cannon, Angel Street, February/March 1988. Since 1970 Associated British Cinemas had no longer been an independent company and in 1985 Thorn EMI decided to sell the film side of the business. It was eventually bought by the Cannon group in May 1986. The Sheffield ABC was given the name Cannon but not until January 1987. Cannon was seeking opportunities to realize some of its assets and sold the cinema to property developers; it closed on 28 July 1988. The premature closure of a splendidly designed cinema was greatly regretted at the time. Most probably the main auditorium could have been subdivided but few would have felt confident in predicting the commercial outcome.

Two

Around the City Centre: Cinemas that also Served

There were eleven 'second run' or specialized cinemas within about a mile of the Town Hall, not counting the Grand Theatre, which closed in 1920. They varied a great deal in location, design, capacity, programme policy and the sort of audience likely to be attracted. The Park and Norfolk Picture Palaces were geographically close to the city centre but functioned as district cinemas relying on their regular customers, most of whom lived in the vicinity; this would also be true of the Coliseum. Although the Don and the Star would also hope to attract local residents, for many years they followed the city centre practice of being open for matinée performances on most afternoons. Quite possibly the hope was that those who had come into town to do some shopping might decide to visit the cinema on their way home. In the early years the Lansdowne also held regular matinées but these were discontinued. As might be expected, the Electra ran continuous performances starting in the early afternoon, a practice that continued during its years as a Classic, while as the News Theatre it had opened mid-morning. The Tivoli in Norfolk Street and the Wicker Picture House were also open on weekday afternoons, as were in later years Cinecenta and the Cineplex/Anvil. The leading picture houses usually ran programmes for at least a full week. The Electra sometimes changed over on a Thursday but as the Classic, programmes ran for seven days. The other cinemas in Sheffield usually changed programmes on a Thursday unless playing a film likely to be particularly popular. The Wicker was not easy to predict, although as Studio 7 (and eventually 5, 6 and 7) films always ran at least six days.

The Electra, Fitzalan Square, opened in February 1911 and closed in November 1982, a span which easily outstrips any other Sheffield cinema. The façade was in glazed terracotta and in the style of fifteenth-century Arabian architecture.

Left: The Classic, November 1963. In 1945 the Electra had been sold to Capital and Provincial News Theatres, who ran it as the Sheffield News Theatre. By the mid-fifties the attraction of newsreels was beginning to fade, the name of the hall being changed to Cartoon Cinema in 1959. The company had for many years operated a small chain of Classic cinemas showing revivals and on 15 January 1962 the Sheffield Classic was born. An extensive face-lift had been carried out but closure had been avoided by doing much of the work at night. The renovations had involved removal of decorative plaster work, while the grimy but rather attractive original façade had been concealed beneath the modern cladding. There was a sophisticated remote control projection system and a new screen but the screen curtains had shrunk while being cleaned, a misfortune hopefully camouflaged by a display of artificial flowers below the screen – eventually the curtains were replaced. Seating capacity had been reduced to 484. In 1963 a Classic children's club was launched with shows on Saturday mornings. It flourished for many years but gradually attendances dropped off with the declining fortunes of the cinema.

Right: A touch of class. The metal handles of the armour-plated entrance doors were fashioned in the form of strips of film. The handles were a replica of those used at the Classic's flagship cinema in Baker Street.

The Classic, April 1973. Many outstanding films had been shown but eventually the supply of vintage 'Classics' began to run out. Cannon, an American company, took over the remnants of the Classic circuit in April 1982. For the Sheffield Classic the writing was already on the wall and the cinema closed on 24 November 1982.

Fitzalan Square, c. 1902. On the right is Wonderland, a wooden fairground-type structure where 'animated pictures' were among the entertainments presented. The projector was mounted on a platform; there was no bottom spool and the film simply fell into a basket and had to be rewound before the next performance. The Electra was built on the site a few years later.

The Electra auditorium. The Electra Palace opened on 10 February 1911. The auditorium was notable for the delicate fibrous plasterwork, the balcony front being embellished with finely modelled cupids. Shaded dome lights illuminated the cupola in the centre of the ceiling, while the hall was lit by reflected light from concealed sources. The platform below the front of the screen was utilized for the display of moss and roses. An unusual feature was the asymmetrical curved balcony. Seats were upholstered and tip-up even in the pit, the cheapest part of the house. Seating capacity was probably about 670. When shares had been offered to the public, the prospectus referred to the building of a cinema with 1,000 seats and at the time of opening the management were understandably reticent in mentioning figures. At circle level there was an attractively furnished tea lounge; tea was evidently regarded as the hallmark of gentility.

In 1929 the Electra jumped the gun and advertised 'Talking Pictures' before the other city centre cinemas were ready to bring in sound. Equipment had been hired from British Phototone, who used a disc recording and provided ten minute shorts of instrumentalists or variety artists. These were shown from March 1929 for some nine weeks before the hall reverted to wholly silent programmes; sound features were not shown until January 1930.

A film ball at the City Hall, November 1949. Dennis Price and Rosamund John are the celebrity guests. The managers are believed to be (from the left) George Reddish (News Theatre), -?-, Bernard Dore (Stocksbridge), Arthur Ollerenshaw (Coliseum, Spital Hill), Bill Brown (Chantrey), Roy Mason (Gaumont) standing behind William Lawton (Dronfield), and Sam Butchart, who was national secretary of the Cinema Managers' Association.

A crowd standing in front of the News Theatre but who are they? A meeting of cinema managers has been suggested but a summer staff outing looks more likely. The man in plus fours on the extreme left may be C.W.A. Potter, chief projectionist at the Don.

The Tivoli, Norfolk Street, December 1921, when the attraction was Chaplin's *The Kid*. Sheffield's first cinema was a converted mission hall and was opened by Jasper Redfern in July 1905 as the Central Hall. The cinema occupied the main hall, which was at ground level, but there was a gallery at first floor level; it provided seating for about 550. Films were interspersed with variety acts. Shows were at 7 p.m. and 9 p.m. with a Saturday children's matinée at 3 p.m., which often attracted long queues; admission was one penny, each child being given a small stick of rock on entry and an orange on leaving. By 1911 Redfern was in financial difficulty and his company wound up. Fortunately new proprietors were able to step in. The hall closed for four months while the balcony was reconstructed and the stage enlarged. From 1914 onwards the hall was known as the Tivoli. Variety acts were becoming more difficult to book because artists were being called up, and in 1915 they were dropped. In the early twenties various improvements were made; a grotto-style décor embellished the vestibule with such features as a miniature lake, statues, fountains and plants. However, there was a serious fire in November 1927 and the hall remained closed for eight months. For a time after it reopened it was called the New Tivoli but the public came to know it as the 'ranch house' because of its reputation for showing westerns, particularly during school holiday periods. In 1932 admission prices were reduced to improve flagging attendances; they were less than when Redfern opened the Central Hall in 1905. The hall was damaged on the first night of the Blitz and never reopened as a cinema.

The Grand Theatre, West Bar, c. 1936. The New Star Music Hall was partly rebuilt and opened as the Grand in 1887; further improvements were carried out in 1893. Although the outside appearance remained undistinguished, the auditorium was quite attractively laid out. Successive managements had struggled to make ends meet when Frank MacNaghten took over in August 1896 with twice-nightly variety, which was a fairly new idea at the time. Although the potential of such a small hall was limited, its acknowledged success was the springboard from which MacNaghten launched his other enterprises. On the crest of the wave in 1910 his empire extended to three theatres, seventeen music halls and two cinemas, most of which were controlled from his Sheffield office. 'Animated pictures' were first shown at the Grand in November 1896, while still a novelty, but only as a short interlude in a variety programme. However, they came to be shown on a more regular basis and from December 1908 the hall was mainly used for films. It ranked as Sheffield's third cinema after the Central Hall, Norfolk Street, and the Theatre Royal, Attercliffe. It closed in 1920 with the intention of building a much larger 'superkinema' on a site that would have involved the demolition of a number of cottages. This was not immediately possible and by the time the housing shortage had eased, the cinema trade in Sheffield was experiencing a disastrous slump. The local authority would not sanction the reopening of the old premises as either a cinema or a music hall, although film trade shows were allowed. However, these ceased in 1924. For a time it was in use as a public house but by the mid-thirties it was semi-derelict. There was never a realistic chance of a new cinema being built but the scheme was not finally abandoned until 1938 when the property was sold to the local authority and demolished.

The Coliseum, Spital Hill, that closed on 2 November 1963; the final programme was a double bill of *The Horse Without a Head* and *Savage Sam*. The cinema had opened on 24 April 1913. Of the 1,400 seats only those in the balcony were upholstered; there was a separate entrance to the pit, where seating was on wooden benches. The front of the balcony was embellished with plaster medallions, surmounted by cherubs and linked by festoons. Suspended from the ceiling were two massive brass electroliers, while the walls were studded with electric lights in the shape of a dragon fly. The attendants wore a uniform of a frock coat made of chocolate-coloured cloth with aluminium braiding. An organ was installed in 1921, built by the Huddersfield firm of Peter Conacher; it was in two parts, placed on opposite sides of the screen. In the twenties the Coliseum matched the leading city centre cinemas in presenting the really big pictures with an augmented orchestra, a range of effects and a vocal accompaniment. There was a small stage, which was enlarged in 1929 to launch a season of cine-variety. However, the public's clamour for talking pictures won the day and the stage was never used again after they were introduced in April 1930. In 1935 a new proscenium was built, the auditorium being redecorated in futuristic style and refurnished throughout with tub chairs. Some damage occurred on the first night of the Sheffield Blitz, rather more than was apparent at the time. Five years later it was found that the ceiling spars were coming away from the main joist and it became necessary to close the cinema for a fortnight. In 1954 a large panoramic screen was installed, although the first film to play in Cinemascope was not shown until November 1955. Unlike the Adelphi, the Coliseum was not equipped to handle Scope prints with a magnetic stereophonic track, having opted for the facility of 'Perspecta' sound, a more basic stereophonic system using two optical tracks.

The Coliseum, Spital Hill, by night. The cinema had always been closely associated with the Gent family; the last manager was Harry Gent, grandson of William Thompson Gent, who for many years was chairman and managing director. Another name linked with the cinema was Arthur J. Ollerenshaw, who was manager from 1918 to 1954.

The Norfolk Picture Palace, September 1959. Sunday opening only started in November 1957 but the films were always different from those shown during the week. Probably the easiest title to identify from the posters is *Forbidden Planet*, which was not shown when originally released but now makes a belated appearance on a Sunday.

The Norfolk Picture Palace, Duke Street, at the Talbot Street junction, September 1959. The cinema opened on Christmas Eve 1914 and closed on Christmas Eve 1959. The architect was Edmund Winder & Co. There was no reference to the opening in the Sheffield press but nearly forty years later the *Sheffield Star* published a remarkable photograph of the poster for the opening show; it had been uncovered in August 1954, when a billboard had been removed. Seating capacity was about 1,000. The term 'balcony', which was still in use in the 1950s, referred to a raised area at the back of the saloon fronted by a red velvet curtain. In 1919 the hall had been given a somewhat more imposing entrance. In 1927 the Norfolk was among the cinemas that obtained a 'Panatrope' to obviate the need for live musicians. This was a gramophone with a double turntable on which records were played using a cue sheet. The first sound film was *The Rainbow Man*, which was shown during Christmas week in 1929. Most probably for reasons of economy the little-known Electrocord system had been installed but by 1932 it had been replaced by Western Electric. In 1937 the hall was modernized under a Friese-Greene contract. This involved remodelling the proscenium, the introduction of concealed lighting and the redecoration of the auditorium in pastel shades. The entrance was fronted by armour-plated glass and a new paybox installed. The walls of the auditorium had been treated to improve acoustic quality and Western Electric's latest 'mirrophonic' sound system added the finishing touch. The hall was one of many cinemas that only opened in the evening but there was a tradition of Saturday children's matinées, which were apt to be rather rowdy, particularly if there was a breakdown. One of the attendants used to have a long prop to reach kids who were misbehaving in the middle of a row; the theory was that a tap on the head would calm them down. Rex Hickman, the manager since 1929, retired on Christmas Eve 1954 after forty years' service; he always seemed very proud of his cinema and was often to be seen greeting regulars wearing spats and a carnation. The first film in Cinemascope was the popular *Three Coins in the Fountain*, which was shown in April 1955. Except for the Palace, Union Street, the Norfolk was the only cinema close to the city centre that showed films in Scope with the enhancement of stereophonic sound.

Sheffield Park Picture Palace, South Street, 1915. It had opened on 1 August 1913 with seats for about 800, including those in the balcony. The façade of the building was in white faience; there was an ornamental parapet linking twin towers, although these were later removed. Conspicuously placed were the letters SPP, which stood for Sheffield Park Pictures. The Park was one of the few Sheffield cinemas that relied on a solo pianist for providing the musical accompaniment to silent films. Sheffield Park Pictures closed the cinema in June 1960 but granted a short term lease to Kerner Entertainments, who for the first time opened the cinema on a Sunday. The Park again closed in June 1962 but it was not quite the end of the story.

The Park, May 1964. Film enthusiast Dennis O'Grady achieved an ambition to run his own cinema when he managed to reopen the Park in November 1963, offering three changes of programme weekly. It finally closed on New Year's Eve 1966 with *Peter Pan* and *Emil and the Detectives*.

The staff of the Park Picture Palace, 1917. John Keaton, the manager, is on the back row wearing a trilby. Percy Brothwell, the Chief Projectionist, is on the left of the back row; he remained at the Park until the early thirties and was later joined by his younger brother Harold. His sister Gladys is on the left of the front row.

The façade of the former Don around 1979, before it had been concealed behind further cladding. Closure of the cinema on 1 March 1958 was most unexpected, for the previous year the hall had been redecorated; additionally, a large new screen had been installed with the latest sound equipment.

The Don Picture Palace, West Bar, as it appeared in a promotional display in the Sheffield press. 'Monday next' was 18 November 1912. The fascia above the entrance was blue and gold. The building was faced with brick but orange-tinted terracotta was used extensively for dressings. There was a novel device operating after dark in which a clown on one side of the entrance appeared to throw a ball of electric lights to a clown on the other side, who in turn threw it on a to a sign which gradually spelt out 'Picture Palace'. The architect was Henry Paterson. Seating accommodation was for around 950. The most expensive seats were in the centre of the auditorium and were plush-covered tip-up chairs: the seats at the back were also tip-up but covered in leatherette, while the cheapest seats at the front were only forms; access to these was from a side entrance. A segmental ceiling was relieved by plaster cornices, ribs and panels. Plasterwork and decoration were carried out by J.L. Harrison, a Sheffield firm that had previously been responsible for the Heeley Palace and the Picturedrome, Grimesthorpe. There were two projectors, a Gaumont 'Maltese Cross' and a specially constructed model, which it was claimed would eliminate all flicker. In 1914 a large balcony was constructed that provided seats for another 350; this was quite a major undertaking that involved raising the roof. The hall reopened in 1914 after redecoration. In 1915 a café and grill room was opened. Further redecoration was carried out in 1917 after the installation of an improved system of ventilation; the saloon was completely refurbished. In the days of the silent cinema the Don followed other city centre cinemas in maintaining quite a large orchestra. In July 1927 Sheffield and District Cinematograph Theatres, proprietors of the Electra, Cinema House and Globe, also acquired the Don. The cinema went over to sound in April 1930, British Acoustic equipment being installed. For some reason this was replaced in 1934 by the Cinephone system but in 1944 the cinema went back to BA after a fire in the projection booth. The Don had followed the path of other city centre cinemas and ran matinées on most afternoons; as late as 1947 there were continuous programmes from 2 p.m. on all afternoons except Fridays. In later years there were matinées on Monday and Thursday but these were discontinued in 1954. The first feature in Scope was in February 1956. In May 1957 the hall closed for redecoration and the installation of an unusually large screen; the first film after reopening was *Oklahoma!*. Since then many a new day may have dawned; but for the Don they were strictly numbered.

Studio 7, May 1972. For the curious, the titles of the films are *Erica – the Performer* and *Sex Service*. The cinema had opened as the Wicker Picture House on 14 June 1920. The exterior was in white faience, the frills including a series of Grecian urns aloft along a parapet. There was a circle, the total seating capacity being 1,080. The hall went over to talking pictures in May 1930; it was the last city centre cinema to do so. The Wicker did not escape the war unscathed; the roof was damaged during the Blitz and the cinema did not reopen until April 1941. It was one of only five Sheffield cinemas that opened when Sunday opening was first permitted in August 1944. In 1962 the frontage was refaced with cedar wood, while above the canopy a blue and white aluminium fascia was surrounded by a large neon sign. The auditorium had been completely stripped and refurnished, the number of rows in the stalls being reduced by a third. The hall reopened as Studio 7 and was billed as the International Film Theatre. And so it was, but it was difficult to predict the type of film likely to be shown from week to week. There were some first-class recent releases; quality foreign films with sub-titles; British or American action films with a title suggestive of sensation, violence or horror; nudist films and undistinguished foreign films, which were usually dubbed and given a salacious title. In the later years rather too many fell into this X-certificate category. Further modernization was carried out in 1967 but shortly afterwards there was a serious fire and the cinema did not reopen for five months. It was 'tripled' in 1974, Studio 5 being a conversion of the stalls and seating 280; Studios 6 and 7 resulted from a division of the circle and seated 110 and 123. The cinema closed in December 1982 but was reopened somewhat optimistically in April 1986 by an independent exhibitor, the programmes being more family orientated; it finally closed on 20 August 1987.

The Star Picture House, Ecclesall Road, at the junction with William Street. The only dating clue is the title *Shanghaied*, a film that never played at the Star but was shown at the Abbeydale on 28-30 March 1929. The Star had opened on 23 December 1915. A feature of the building was an ornamental dome supported by nine columns; there were also a series of Grecian urns projecting above a low parapet that carried round the whole of the street frontage. There was a balcony, the total seating capacity being 1,028. The proprietors were Sheffield Premier Pictures but there was a restructuring of the company in 1929 with the emergence of new directors and a severance of previous links with the Abbeydale and Central Picture Houses. During the first night of the Sheffield Blitz there was a direct hit on the projection booth. Fortunately the bomb failed to explode but there was serious damage to the roof and other parts of the building. The hall remained closed for nearly ten months, reopening on 6 October 1941. It was not until fourteen years later that the stalls and circle lounges were fully restored. In 1955 the Star for the first time became a Star Cinema. The omens for a successful partnership seemed propitious but in 1962 the end came suddenly. Bingo had been launched so successfully that after only two trial sessions the Star management decided to close the cinema forthwith; this was on 17 January 1962. It remained a bingo hall until 1984.

The former Star cinema in December 1974, when Star bingo was the name of the game. The colonnaded tower and other ornamental trappings were removed in 1941 following air-raid damage.

Living pictures at the Sheffield Market fairground, c. 1900. Randall Williams brought his booth to Sheffield's Christmas fair in 1897. Thomas Payne, John Proctor and Enoch Farrar were among the showmen who followed. Travelling picture palaces were sometimes quite elaborate with expensive mechanical organs. By 1914 fairground bioscope shows were on their way out.

Another early bioscope show on the Smithfield fairground. 'Captain' T. Payne was one of several leading showmen who toured the fairs; he eventually opened a picture palace in his home town of Ashton-under-Lyne.

Preparing the site off Devonshire Street to receive the Cinerama Touring Theatre. This vast inflatable tent was centrally heated and provided seating for 1,000; the screen was 103ft wide and 37ft deep. Three linked projectors each provided a segment of the ultra-wide screen. 'This is Cinerama' opened on 6 February 1965; three months later the show moved on.

The former Lansdowne Picture Palace, London Road, at the junction with Boston Street, in 1989, when it was the Locarno dance hall. It opened on or about 18 December 1914. The building was notable for a terracotta façade in green and white with a pagoda-style entrance. There was quite a large balcony with a total seating capacity approaching 1,500, but the conditions would have been rather cramped; by 1940 it had been reduced to 940. Music was provided by a 'bijou' orchestra of seven but the orchestra blossomed in the 1920s with some twelve musicians at evening performances. Although retaining its identity, Lansdowne Pictures was closely associated with Hallamshire Cinemas, one of Sheffield's three local circuits. The cinema abruptly closed following the air-raid on the night of 12 December 1940, although it was only slightly damaged. It is difficult to resist the conclusion that the proprietors received offers from displaced stores that were too good to refuse. During the war years it was occupied by Marks and Spencer. Even after the war it remained in use as a department store. From 1954 it became a dance hall and has since been used as a night club under a variety of names.

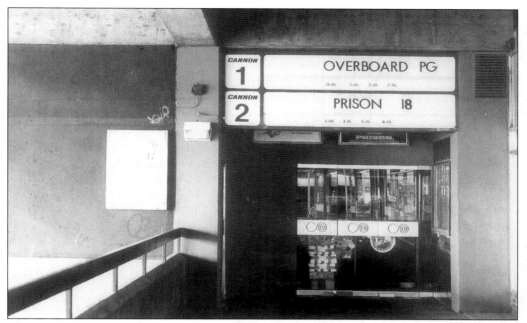

The entrance to Cinecenta (now Cannon) in June 1988: the horizontal panels of the door frames still carry the Cinecenta logo. Cinecenta opened on 30 January 1969; twin auditoria were included within the Pond Street multi-storey complex. The entrance to Cinecenta was through aluminium-framed plate-glass doors. The paybox was to the right, the parallel stairways being on the left. The outer of these led to Cinecenta 1, which seated 141, and the inner to Cinecenta 2, the larger auditorium, with 190 seats. There was a second paybox on the stairway to Cinecenta 1 but this was only used when one auditorium was open to the public and the other was restricted to club members. There was a projection booth for each auditorium but both were rather cramped and the projection beam was relayed by a system of mirrors; the projectors were Philips FP 20s. The stated intention was to show films of specialized interest that were unlikely to be booked by the major circuits but such a declaration proved to less transparent that it appeared. From March 1969 Cinecenta 2 became the home of the 'Penthouse Cineclub', which was able to show uncensored films on a membership basis. For a few months Cinecenta 1 remained open to the general public but from October 1969 a 'members only' policy operated in both auditoria. However, from October 1971 Cinecenta 1 was again open to the general public and for some ten years co-existed with the 'Penthouse Cineclub' in Cinecenta 2. From September 1981 admission to Cinecenta 1 was again restricted to club members but from October 1982 all restrictions were lifted, although the programmes were well sprinkled with X certificates. Cinecenta was acquired by Star Cinemas in 1972 and in 1985 by Cannon; in May 1986 it was renamed the Cannon, Flat Street. After Cannon had decided to close the cinema in early 1989, Rank Theatres surprisingly expressed an interest and eventually acquired the lease, renaming the cinema the Fiesta in August 1989. While the Fiesta closed on 29 September 1991, the auditoria were incorporated within the Odeon 7 multiplex.

The Anvil, November 1988. My *Girlfriend's Boyfriend* was a French film shown with English subtitles. The Cineplex opened on 31 January 1972, the shells of the auditoria being derived from three shop units. The main snag was that they were never completely soundproof. David Williams had graduated to the higher tiers of cinema management within the Rank Organization but was looking for an opportunity to branch out on his own. In the early years Cineplex was limited to the use of 16mm projectors, which restricted the choice of new films. Later a 35mm projector was installed to serve the largest auditorium. Williams was his own manager and brought a personal touch to bear in relating to the film-going public. Audience support for the more popular films enabled him to book subtitled and other films with a minority appeal. However, after twelve years, he decided to call it a day and Cineplex closed in February 1983.

In association with the British Film Institute, Sheffield City Council had pioneered the concept of a Sheffield Film Theatre in 1967, taking over the Library Theatre for a monthly 'film week'. On the closure of Cineplex the authority had been persuaded to take over the lease and operate it as a civic enterprise. While it was reopened almost immediately, it was not until the autumn that the venture was re-launched as the Anvil with a more structured programme policy. After some work had been carried out on the frontage to give it a rather more distinctive appearance, it reopened on 6 October 1983. Seating capacities were 110 in 1, 76 in 2 and 65 in 3, a total of 251. In 1985 the third auditorium was closed for nearly three months in order to install a second 35mm projector and carry out other improvements. The Anvil survived for a period approaching eight years but somewhat precariously. Faced with mounting financial pressures, it caused regret but little surprise when the cinema closed on 3 November 1990.

Three

The East End Cinemas

The East End is a fairly well-defined territory and included the Attercliffe theatres, the Palace and the Theatre Royal; the Globe, the Pavilion and the Regal; the Darnall Cinema, the Darnall Picture Palace (more commonly known as the Balfour) and the Lyric; the Picturedrome (later Regent Theatre) and the Victory in Upwell Street; and the Palaces at Tinsley and Wincobank. The Attercliffe Palace operated as a cinema from 1909 to 1919 and from 1930 to 1937, while the Theatre Royal, Attercliffe, was mainly a cinema from 1907 until it closed in 1933. The Picturedrome was a cinema from 1912 to 1925 and from 1930 to 1934, but it then reverted to being a variety hall until it closed in 1940. The Regal opened in 1935 with cine-variety but within a few months live acts were dropped except as occasional events. The remaining halls never set out to be anything other than cinemas, although the Adelphi sometimes booked turns during the 1920s.

Sheffield exhibitors had come to terms with the fact that admission prices at East End cinemas were generally lower than in other parts of the city. Many of the cinemas had been built in the boom years before the First World War and most families looking to have a night out had plenty to choose from within a convenient distance of their homes. The Adelphi was regarded as Attercliffe's posh cinema but the Pavilion also had its attractions. Those who had a favourite cinema would still be prepared to go elsewhere, if the word got round that there was a good film on. The cinemas in the East End were well supported, at least until television took over in the 1950s. Another adverse factor in later years was the depopulation of Attercliffe as a result of housing clearance schemes.

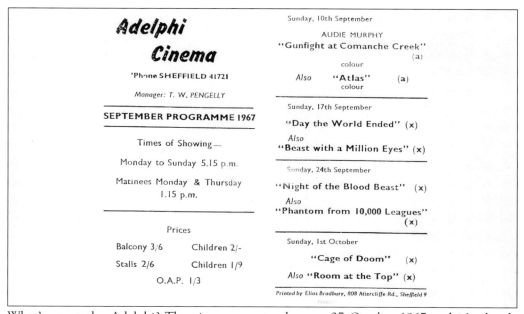

What's on at the Adelphi? The cinema was to close on 27 October 1967 and it's already September. The monthly programme was printed on a card but the side setting out the weekly films has not been reproduced.

The former Adelphi Picture Theatre, Vicarage Road, Attercliffe, in 1988, while still a bingo club. The building was of red brick supported by reinforced concrete with buff and blue terracotta enrichments on the façade. Above the main entrance was a small turret dome in faience; stained-glass windows were also a feature. The Adelphi opened on 18 October 1920. Seating capacity including the balcony was 1,350. The auditorium was decorated to a Wedgewood design with green panels. The projection booth was at ground level. The screen was at the same end of the hall as the entrance: somewhat unusually it was made entirely of three-ply wood and was on rollers, so that it could be moved back to provide a stage. Variety turns were included in some programmes, while from time to time a silent feature would be presented with an augmented orchestra and singers. The hall went over to sound in March 1930; it was likely that the screen would have been replaced as the stage was no longer in use. In 1936 the hall closed for a week, all seating being replaced, the flooring relaid and 'Holophane' lighting introduced. Around the same time a car park was provided for the use of customers. In August 1939 the hall closed for redecoration and the installation of Western Electric's 'mirrophonic' sound system. The cinema was damaged on the second night of the Blitz but reopened a month later. In August 1946 the hall closed for four weeks for renovation. A panoramic screen was installed in January 1954, while in March 1955 Cinemascope was launched with the fringe benefit of magnetic stereo-sound. The Adelphi had only four managers: Abraham Taylor, Donald Clark, George Reddish and Trevor Pengally. And only two managing directors: William Thompson Gent, who died in 1930, and Herbert Oliver. There remained a close association with the Coliseum on Spital Hill and both cinemas introduced Sunday opening on the same weekend in October 1955. The hall closed on 28 October 1967. It has since been 'listed' Grade II as a building of special architectural or historical importance.

The Tinsley Picture Palace, Sheffield Road, August 1926. A balcony seating 120 had just been constructed, while the hall had been redecorated and largely refurnished. The Palace opened on 16 November 1912, when Tinsley was still in Rotherham. Seating capacity was about 600 but some of it would have been on forms. In October 1919 the cinema was bought by the Wincobank Picture Palace Company. By April 1920 extensive alterations were nearing completion; these included the building up of the frontage, which previously had only extended to single-storey level on the flanks; some 150 seats had been added to the capacity of the hall. In August 1922 there was a fire in the projection booth but this was quickly brought under control. Until 1924 the cinema had relied on a pianist for musical accompaniments but a trio was then engaged and from 1926 a small orchestra. John Madin was a pianist for a time before going as organist to the Heeley Palace. Talking pictures came to Tinsley in April 1930, Western Electric equipment being installed. In 1938 the Palace was reported to be the first cinema in Yorkshire to be equipped with the more powerful alternating current arc lamps. Since 1930 the Tinsley and Wincobank Palaces had been operated through separate companies, although the businesses remained interrelated and under the control of the Wadsworth family. In 1950 the hall closed for three weeks while various repairs were undertaken. During the fifties suburban cinemas found it increasingly difficult to break even and rowdyism could be a problem. Cinemascope brought in audiences for a while, the first feature being *The Robe* in March 1955. The cinema never opened on Sundays nor sought solace in bingo. It closed on 15 February 1958.

The Tinsley Palace, August 1926. From left to right: Leonard Victor Wadsworth, John William Wadsworth (who died in 1930), Leonard Downes Wadsworth (manager), Mrs Lloyd (paybox cashier). The façade is quite elaborate, with glazed terracotta arranged in vertical segments.

A closer view of Victor Wadsworth, Mrs Lloyd and Leonard Wadsworth. Victor assisted his father in various capacities before eventually becoming chief projectionist but he did not become manager of the Tinsley Palace until after his father's death in 1946. Victor Wadsworth was still at the helm when the Palace closed in 1958.

Wincobank Picture Palace, off Fife Street, around 1948, when there were still post-war restrictions on the use of paper for billposting. The Palace had opened on 11 June 1914. The hall was mainly constructed of brick, the front elevation carrying terracotta and stone facings. The entrance had a mosaic floor and was approached up a rather steep flight of steps. The seating capacity was 550. The projection booth was on the first floor; a single Butcher's No. 12 projector had been installed which was cranked by hand. Electricity for lighting the hall was generated using a gas engine; a public electricity supply was not extended to Fife Street until 1921. Some alterations and improvements were made in 1919 and the cinema was redecorated. In July 1926 the cinema closed for four weeks, mainly to install a balcony, the scheme being similar to that being undertaken at the Tinsley Palace; the paybox was repositioned, while the auditorium was redecorated and largely refurnished. The balcony increased capacity by some 100 seats. By the mid-twenties the musical accompaniment was provided by a trio of pianist, violinist and either a drummer or trumpeter; it could well be that in earlier times there was only a piano. 'Talkies' arrived in April 1930, Western Electric equipment being installed. After the Second World War it closed for redecoration in 1946, during the last week in July. The cinema was again closed at this time of year between 1947 and 1949 but only to enable staff to take their holiday at a time when business was traditionally slack. The practice was then discontinued but in August 1953 the hall took a week off for 'modernization', the work involving the construction of a new proscenium flanked by splay walls, improvements to ventilation and lighting and the installation of a modern paybox. The first film in Cinemascope was *The Robe*, which opened in March 1955. In the 1950s the Thursday and later the Monday matinées were dropped but the Saturday children's matinée was retained. The Palace closed on 21 February 1959, having outlasted its sister hall at Tinsley by twelve months.

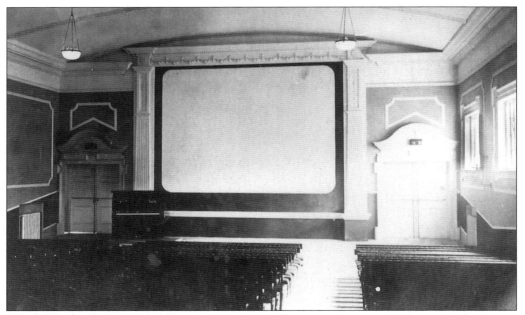

The Wincobank Palace auditorium, c. 1914. The proscenium arch is simple but quite attractive. Screen curtains were an innovation for a later age. A piano was for today.

The Wincobank Palace auditorium, c. 1914. The comfortable seats were at the back of the house and upholstered in blue. Further forward the bench-type seating looks rather Spartan but there were back rests and it was covered in red plush. Lighting was by means of four large reflex clusters hung by bronze chains, four centre lights and several side brackets, which gave a ruby glow.

The Wincobank Palace, c. 1923. Cyril (Frederick) Wadsworth, the figure on the left of the back row, succeeded his father as manager in 1922. The only other person identified is the schoolgirl, Muriel Wadsworth. Cyril Wadsworth soldiered on as manager until his death in 1947. He was followed by his son (Henry) Alvery Wadsworth. From 1957 he became heavily involved on the projection side and delegated many of the managerial tasks to his sister Muriel.

The former Wincobank Public Baths, then a community centre, in 1992. The portrayal of the Palace was one of a number of wall paintings depicting various aspects of the life of the local community.

The Darnall Picture Palace, Staniforth Road, at the junction with Balfour Road, c. 1914. This was the first of Darnall's three cinemas and opened on 19 July 1913. The architect was Walter G. Buck. The building was in the style of a mock castle, a number of electric torches enhancing the effect by night. Seating capacity was about 750. A Gaumont and a Pathé projector had been installed. It had opened with a ladies' bijou orchestra but by August 1915 there was only a piano accompaniment. From December 1921 the Darnall Picture Palace became a hall operated by Hallamshire Cinemas, which was one of three local circuits. There was a small stage and turns appear to have been booked from time to time, but details are lacking for the Darnall Picture Palace seldom advertised in the local press until the later thirties. Those interested would no doubt have scanned the billboards and known which of the local shops displayed the week's cinema programmes. From the trade journals it is apparent that the first sound films were not shown until April 1931, which for Sheffield was quite late in the day. The building was damaged on the second night of the Sheffield Blitz but reopened on 13 January 1941. In October 1955 a new wide screen was installed but the first presentation in Cinemascope was not until July 1956. The first Sunday show was in September 1955, performances continuing until the hall closed, which was on 28 February 1959.

Below opposite: The photograph of staff at the Darnall Cinema appears to have been taken in the 1930s. William Brindley, the proprietor and manager, is missing but the others have been identified as, from left, Ethel Haughton, Arnold Roberts, Phoebe Clayton, -?-, Mr Haughton, Evelyn Trickett, Myra Palmer. Arnold Roberts came as a chocolate boy on leaving school but he was soon recruited as assistant projectionist, eventually being promoted chief, a position he retained until the cinema closed in 1957. It was not a coincidence that the last film to be shown was Henry Fonda and James Cagney in *Mr Roberts*.

Another view of the Darnall Picture Palace, *c.* 1928. The main entrance was arched and situated at the road junction corner; it was set beneath a plaque of ornamentally engraved terracotta and impressively flanked by pinnacled buttresses. There was a pit entrance to the front of the auditorium off Balfour Road. In 1920 there was a major reconstruction involving raising the height of the roof and carrying the auditorium further back. A balcony of some fifteen rows was installed, which was unusual in that it did not hang over the seats in the saloon but was constructed behind them. Seating was increased to just under a thousand. Stanley Swindells came to the cinema in 1928 and became one of Sheffield's longest serving managers, although he left shortly before the cinema closed. There is some uncertainty as to when the hall began calling itself the Balfour – presumably this was the name already widely used by those living in the vicinity. The name was referred to in a year book published early in 1934, although the hall continued to be licensed as the Darnall Picture Palace until the time it closed.

The Darnall Cinema, Catcliffe Road, at the junction with Hazel Road, July 1955. The arched entrance led to the vestibule and paybox but less conspicuous is the entry on the right, which was to the pit. The cinema had opened on 15 September 1913. The projection booth was positioned above the ground floor level; for many years entry was only possible up a ladder from the rewind room below. The original proprietor was George Payling, a local builder, but finding that his sons were not interested in going into the business he leased the hall to William Forsdike and in July 1920 to William Charles Brindley of the Sheffield Film Service, a rental agency; Brindley was later able to buy the cinema on favourable terms. Until 1954 he managed the hall himself with the help of his sons, Vaughan, Stuart and Frederick. In 1929 the projection booth and rewind room were enlarged. Access was now via a passage at the side of the cinema. Although it was external and involved climbing steps, it was easier to negotiate than the internal route up a ladder. An incidental benefit was that there was slightly more space at the back of the hall and the seating could be re-spaced to give a little more leg room. Of the sons, Vaughan's main contribution was on the technical side. Working with the 'Vitavox' company, he had devised a system of sound reproduction suitable for both sound on film and disc recording; 'Vitavox' equipment was still used in the 1950s. Saturday children's matinées had been held fairly regularly during the post-war period, while from 1952 afternoon matinées were revived on Monday and Thursday. As audiences dwindled, sales of ice cream became of increasing economic importance. In a single record-breaking day, even the smallest show in Sheffield managed to sell 144 dozen tubs. The Darnall Cinema closed on 2 November 1957; it was only the third cinema to close since the casualties of the 1940 Blitz.

The Royal Picture House, Staniforth Road, close to the junction with Attercliffe Road, c. 1925. The cinema was a converted industrial building that opened on Boxing Day 1896 as the People's Theatre, Attercliffe. It was renamed the Theatre Royal, Attercliffe, on 13 December 1897. Drama was presented through a succession of touring companies, although pantomime, musical comedy and very occasionally vaudeville were also staged. The theatre closed in May 1899 for major reconstruction and remained closed for over six months, while the balcony was extended, the pit and stalls enlarged and the stage reconstructed. The probability is that seating capacity was increased from 750 to around 1,100. The theatre operated as a drama house for a number of years but throughout the summer of 1906 only films were shown. Indeed from 9 February 1907 it was mainly in use as a cinema, although the pictures were often supported by a singer appearing on stage. From 1909 onward a variety act might appear instead of a singer, and a comedian or comedienne was quite common. For over three months in 1909 the Royal demonstrated 'Cinephone', an early talking picture device. In 1913 it was one of the few Sheffield cinemas to screen a programme in Kinemacolor, an early colour process that required a special projector. The Royal continued to book variety artists throughout the war years when most Sheffield cinemas had dropped variety acts. However, from August 1919 live performers only appeared occasionally. In September 1927 and again during Christmas week singing shorts introduced the novelty of sound in support of a silent feature. The first full-length feature was *Movietone Follies*, which was shown in September 1929. It was the fourth Sheffield hall to go over to sound and the first in Attercliffe. The Royal continued to show sound films but closed on 17 June 1933.

The Regal, Attercliffe Road, May 1954. The new cinema retained some of the external walls of the Theatre Royal but the reconstruction involved considerable rebuilding. The architect was Harold J. Shepherd. There was now an imposing façade notable for the extensive use of glass. The architraves to the doorway were constructed in black toughened glass; above these were primrose squares with green decorative horizontal lines. The face of the canopy had been treated in primrose and red vitrolite. Glass was also used for auditorium decoration in the form of green mirrors with black skirting. The interior work was carried out or supervised by Kalee Ltd under an all-in contract that included decoration, fibrous plaster, electrical fitments, seating and stage and door curtains. A new balcony had been constructed but the hall's seating capacity of 918 remained slightly less than that of the Theatre Royal, although more waiting space had been provided. A stage had been retained but had been reduced in depth to only 11ft. Projection was on the ground floor with Western Electric 'wide range' sound equipment and Kalee No. 11 projectors. The Regal opened on 14 October 1935 and all seemed set for the hall to run on cine-variety lines – as indeed it did during the first ten weeks. Unexpectedly the hall was then leased to the Salford-based J.F. Emery circuit which had other priorities. As a concession possibly to local feelings there were occasional stage presentations mainly during 'birthday weeks' in October 1936, 1937, 1938 and 1940. The cinema was damaged on the second night of the Blitz and did not reopen until 10 March 1941. In August 1944 the Regal was one of the few cinemas to take advantage of the city council's decision to allow Sunday opening. In March 1955 Star Cinemas took over the Emery halls and in May the Regal closed for 'modernization', reopening a week later equipped to show films in Cinemascope. Any respite was temporary and the final curtain fell on Sunday 27 May 1961.

The Attercliffe Palace, Attercliffe Road, c. 1948. The hall opened as the Alhambra Theatre of Varieties on 3 January 1898. The lower part of the frontage was of faience resting on a base of coloured glazed bricks. Above this level the central part of the façade was surfaced with ornamental stucco, while the flanking portions were of red brick. These marked the staircase towers, each terminating in a lead cupola and flag staff. The interior was decorated with a Moorish design. There was a spacious balcony, total seating being about 1,200. From the outset the Alhambra was less successful than the directors and investors had hoped. The company offered a fifteen year lease to T. Allan Edwardes of Derby, a well known theatrical entrepreneur. After the installation of improved heating and undergoing some renovation, the hall reopened in August 1904 as the Attercliffe Palace and continued to run as a twice-nightly variety theatre. The Palace soon settled into a groove as Attercliffe's variety theatre but suddenly all was to change when Edwardes disposed of the lease to the Raymond Animated Picture Company. Matt Raymond signalled a change of direction by showing an all-film programme in June 1909. For a time the hall was advertised as Raymond's Picture Palace: it was Sheffield's fourth cinema but there was usually a vocalist and possibly a turn in support. In November 1911 the Palace changed its name back to the Palace of Varieties and greater play was made of the variety content of the shows. Throughout the war years a combination of pictures and variety was presented without any discernible change in course when Messrs Walker and Bennett took over the lease in September 1916. However, by 1919 the number of acts booked was increasing and audiences were coming to see vaudeville as the main attraction. The Palace was a variety and revue theatre throughout the twenties but it closed in June 1930. After refurbishment it reopened as a 'talkie' cinema on 13 October, showing only films. Towards the end of 1933 there were signs of a change in policy, for from time to time live performers were engaged to bolster a possibly weak feature film. In 1935 there was a Christmas pantomime, followed shortly afterwards by two other shows without films. Thereafter, variety seemed to fall out of favour and for most of 1936, continuing into 1937, only films were shown. Yet the Palace was to close as a cinema on 17 July 1937. It reopened on August Bank Holiday as 'Sheffield's East End Theatre' with seven variety acts. It closed on 1 July 1955 with the revue Strip, Sauce and Spice. This final chapter proved the longest in the theatre's chequered history.

The former Lyric Picture House, Main Road, Darnall, c. 1963. The Lyric opened on 22 November 1920. Although Elisha Clayton was managing director of the Lyric company, the cinema was never brought within the ambit of Heeley and Amalgamated Cinemas. The steel-framed brick building was of quite an attractive appearance with terracotta relief to the façade. The site sloped upward to Fisher Lane, the screen being at the front of the building and the projection booth on the ground floor. There were stairways leading up on both sides of the paybox, giving access to a rather narrow balcony foyer; from here the balcony seats were approached by open passageways leading along both sides of the auditorium. Seating capacity was 1,020 of which 220 seats were in the balcony. The first manager was Henry Lacey, a retired police inspector. After just under a year he accepted a post at one of Clayton's cinemas in the Isle of Man but returned to the Lyric in 1922 and stayed another eight years. The first 'talkie' was *Sunny Side Up*, shown in May 1930. Kalee projectors were used in conjunction with BTH sound equipment, which had been installed following the construction of a rewinding room. Star Cinemas gained control of the Lyric towards the end of 1943. It was the first Sheffield hall to be acquired by Star Cinemas, although the Palace, Stocksbridge, was already in the fold. Early advantage was taken of the opportunity to open on Sundays, performances starting in October 1944; it was the third cinema to open on Sundays outside the city centre. Most Star Cinemas organized Saturday matinées for children and the Lyric was no exception. In March 1954 a panoramic screen was installed, the claim being made that it was the largest in Sheffield's East End. The first film in Cinemascope was shown in May 1955. The last Sunday performance was on 20 May 1962, bingo being introduced the following Sunday; there was also a bingo session on a weekday evening. The hall closed as a cinema on 29 August 1962, reopening the next day as the Star bingo club.

The former Picturedrome, Upwell Street, Grimesthorpe, 1965. It had opened on 18 March 1912. The site was rather cramped but it was quite an attractive brick building faced with stone around arched entrances. A somewhat raised area at the back of the pit was described as the pit circle and offered more comfortable seating than the benches in the cheaper parts of the house; there was also a small balcony. Seating capacity was about 700. By the end of 1912 variety acts were being included in the film programmes. In March 1924 the hall was sold to a syndicate headed by Frederick Phoenix. As cine-variety was the policy at the Phoenix Theatre, there appeared to be scope for running the two cinemas in tandem and one of the sons was installed as manager at the Picturedrome. However, in April 1925 Phoenix leased it to a Manchester syndicate, who reopened it as the Regent Theatre on 4 May 1925. It was quite well suited to being used as a variety and revue theatre, as there was a 16ft deep stage and four dressing rooms; a stage entrance had been constructed in 1916. A concert party booking in May 1929 brought the curtain down on this part of the story. After quite a long intermission, the Picturedrome/Regent was leased to East of England Cinemas and reopened, probably in December 1930; the sound system installed was British Talking Pictures (BTP). By March 1931 the company was in voluntary liquidation but the cinema remained open. In July 1932 the Phoenix family sold the hall to Barnsley Electric Theatre, a small company controlled by Frank and John Eshelby, who were Sheffield builders with a financial interest in the Wicker syndicate. In 1935 the Eshelbys formed a new company, Regent (Varieties) Sheffield, and ran the Regent as a twice-nightly variety and revue theatre from 6 May 1935. No local reference has been traced but a report in the trade press stated that the cinema had been closed for several months. So that marked the end of the Picturedrome. The Regent survived but not without moments of high drama; the theatre closed on 15 June 1940.

The Victory Palace, Upwell Street, 1931. The picture of cleaners outside the cinema entrance was taken by John Payne, a projectionist. Their names were noted as Frances Skelton, Jenny Ashton, Mrs Heard and Lizzie Truelove. The Victory opened on 27 October 1921. The external appearance was undistinguished but the interior was quite attractive. From the road 'Victory' could be made out in red coloured glass, illuminated at night. Seating capacity was 849 including 302 in the balcony. There was a separate pit entrance but even inside the main entrance there were two payboxes, one of which dispensed balcony tickets. The balcony steps divided and led to a comfortable lounge. Among the attractions of the balcony were pairs of double seats on each row; these were to the left of the central aisles, when facing the screen. A single manual organ had been installed; it was a 'Clavorchester' built by the Sheffield firm of Brindley and Foster. For a number of years the organist was J. Percy Hall, who both accompanied the films and gave recitals. Escalating building costs had been a heavy drain on the company's financial reserves and by 1924 it was in serious difficulty, being eventually wound up. In January 1925 the hall was bought by a syndicate of Leeds exhibitors. During most of 1928 the cinema was managed by Barney, son of Max Goldstone, who was one of the exhibitors that still had a financial interest in the business. Early in 1929 Harry Lee was brought in as manager and he remained until 1933. However, from July 1929 control was taken over by Jacob Bickler, who was also a member of the original syndicate. When Lee left, Bickler appointed his son Harry as manager but both the father and his other son Nathaniel were actively involved in the running of the cinema; all commuted from Leeds. Western Electric sound equipment had been installed in April 1930 but silent films were still shown at children's Saturday matinées. The hall opened on Sundays from March 1946 until shortly before the cinema closed, which was on 6 July 1957. The Victory was only the fourth Sheffield cinema to close since the casualties of 1940.

The Pavilion, Attercliffe Common, *c*. 1972, when it was showing Asian films. Built by the proprietors of the Heeley Palace, it opened on 23 December 1915. Above the entrance canopy were four pilasters surfaced in glazed terracotta, while below the parapet at roof level the words music – the pavilion – drama were embossed on inset panels. The auditorium was decorated in Tudor style with oak panelling; there were five boxes on each side. Seating capacity was around 1,250 including the balcony. In 1930 a series of improvements were carried out but the hall did not close. The Pavilion suffered some damage on the first night of the Blitz but had reopened by 23 January 1941. Some fourteen years later it was one of the halls involved when Star Cinemas took over the Heeley and Amalgamated circuit. In January 1955 it closed for 'complete modernization', a term used to cover any redecoration or other work thought necessary, including the replacement of obsolete or faulty equipment. Nor was time lost in applying to the licensing authority with a view to Sunday opening and the holding of Saturday children's matinées. From 1956 the cinema was also open on Sunday afternoons when the hall was hired out to various Asian film societies. In 1961 bingo sessions were introduced for the first time but the story was to take some unexpected twists. In June 1963 the Pavilion closed as a cinema, apart from Saturday afternoon children's matinées. It immediately opened as a casino but from September it went back to being a cinema without roulette or bingo. The Pavilion continued in use as a cinema for nearly five years but returned to bingo in August 1968. In March 1970 the hall was reopened by Elite Cinemas, a Birmingham firm. Asian films were shown on a Sunday and English language films during the week. However, these were discontinued on 24 October 1970, the hall being then mainly used for screening Pakistani films. In 1971 it was refurnished and new projectors installed. The Pavilion remained in use as an Asian cinema until 1979.

The Globe Picture Hall, Attercliffe Common, at the junction with Kirkbridge Road, *c.* 1914. The poster promises 'all picture entertainment'. It was a Saturday, when there was a children's matinée. The Globe, with seating for 1,700, had opened on 10 February 1913 and was the largest cinema to be built in Sheffield until the Regent in 1927. Around roof level was a globe, which at night revolved and emitted constantly changing coloured lights. There was an imposing main staircase with terrazzo steps leading to the balcony and an adjoining tea room. There was ample waiting space in each part of the house so as to avoid queuing in the street. Indeed it was a rather cavernous place with shadowy anterooms on the way to the balcony, which were quite confusing. It also seemed difficult to keep the place clean and by the less respectful was referred to as the 'bug hut'. The Globe was built by the proprietors of the Sheffield Picture Palace but in 1919 it was sold to Sheffield and District Cinematograph Theatres. The hall remained closed for three months so as to improve ventilation and upgrade toilet facilities. Percy Hayward was the new manager; he remained at the Globe for thirty-six years and possibly longer. In 1925 the hall was redecorated and largely refurnished, while in 1938 it closed for three weeks for extensive refurbishment. Unlike most East End cinemas it never opened on Sundays. It closed on 29 June 1959.

Four

Hillsborough and Walkley Cinemas

Away from the city centre, the Phoenix Theatre and the Hillsborough Kinema House were two of only six purpose-designed cinemas that had opened by the end of 1912. To these would be added the Hillsborough Park Cinema, which opened early in 1921. The first hall in Hillsborough to be used as a cinema was the rather high-sounding Palace of Varieties, opened by Joseph Brothwell in February 1909. Another picture and variety house was the Walkley Electric Theatre in Fulton Road, which opened in March 1911. Both would find it difficult to keep up with the opposition, although the Walkley hall survived until 1916. In the meanwhile the Walkley Palladium had opened in December 1914. Although owned by different companies, the Hillsborough Kinema and the Walkley Palladium became closely associated.

The Phoenix Theatre poses a problem. Apart from a picture that appeared in press reports of its opening on 27 March 1911, no photograph has been traced. The Phoenix was the third hall in Sheffield to be designed as a cinema but the intention was to show variety turns as well as films. Seating was probably no more than 640 including the balcony. At the time of opening the stage was 12ft deep but was later extended to 22ft. The first manager was Harold Phoenix, who had been associated with Jasper Redfern at the Central Hall. Unfortunately he died in 1918 as a result of the influenza outbreak and was succeeded by his brother Cecil. From 1925 the hall became a theatre, mainly staging revues, although there were some Saturday film matinées for children. The Phoenix reopened as a cinema on 7 August 1933 after the installation of new projectors and sound equipment. The days of variety were over. Towards the end of 1956 the Phoenix was sold to the proprietors of the Hillsborough Kinema and shortly afterwards Cecil Phoenix retired. The hall closed on 10 September 1960.

The Walkley Palladium, c. 1916. There had always been a close relationship between the Walkley Palladium and the Hillsborough Kinema. The halls usually booked the same films; in 1929 they had both gone over to sound within one week of one another and replaced the equipment at the same time in 1938 with Western Electric's latest system. In September 1945 the Palladium closed for a week for cleaning and redecoration, while the Kinema closed twelve months later but for three weeks. Both closed for a week in June 1951 for redecoration; both went over to Sunday opening on 17 May 1953. Cinemascope arrived a few weeks later at the Palladium but both were equipped to screen prints carrying stereophonic sound on a magnetic track.

The Walkley Palladium, South Street, at the junction with Highton Road, c. 1916. The façade was relieved with imitation stone dressings and pilasters, while ornamental stucco was used extensively in the auditorium. It opened on 17 December 1914, seating capacity being around 1,000; individual upholstered tip-up seats had been installed in all parts of the house. A balcony extended along three sides of the auditorium. Two Kalee projectors were installed. The opening programme included *Brewster's Millions*, a cartoon, topical news and war sketches caricaturing the Kaiser. There was an orchestra of six. Performances were at 6.50 p.m. and 9 p.m. with Saturday matinées at 2.30 p.m. The first manager was W. Vivian Nelson, who stayed until 1917. Among the later managers Jonathan W. Dickinson was in post from 1921 until his death in 1927. He was succeeded by Frederick W. Woodward, who had previously been chief projectionist. The cinema went over to 'talkies' on 25 November 1929; it was the sixth in Sheffield to be wired for sound and the fourth to install the Western Electric system. The first sound film was *The Rainbow Man*, which was a popular choice at the time. Various improvements were carried out over the next two years, culminating in an extensive scheme of redecoration, in which hand painted Lakeland scenes were incorporated. The moulding of the ceiling was painted crimson and gold; six lanterns were suspended, shaded in lemon and pink. In 1935 the hall was refurnished and new tub-seats installed. Colin Arnold was appointed manager when Woodward retired shortly after the end of the war but moved to the Plaza in 1957. The custom for many years had been to hold matinées on Mondays and Thursdays but to these were added Saturday afternoon children's matinées, which were held from February 1958 to July 1960. Sunday opening had been introduced in May 1953 but in May 1962 films made way for a Sunday evening bingo session. However, the cinema closed on 6 October 1962 with a double bill of *Tiara Tahiti* with James Mason and *Gaolbreak* with John Mills.

The Walkley Palladium, *c.* 1950. The figure standing in front of the box office is Arthur Norton, the chief projectionist, who remained in post until the hall closed in 1962. In May 1950 he received a cheque for £25 from the company chairman in recognition of his twenty five years at the cinema; the small ceremony was attended by Vivian Nelson, the first manager at the Palladium.

The Walkley Palladium, June 1950. The steps still look rather steep. The film is *You Can't Sleep Here*, the British title of *I Was a Male War Bride*: it starred Cary Grant and Ann Sheridan. Cinemas still showed photographs as part of their advertising display.

The former Hilllsborough Palace of Varieties, Bradfield Road, c. 1965. A programme of up to seven short films and two or three turns were offered. It could not compete with the Phoenix Theatre and closed in May 1911.

The Hillsborough Park Cinema vestibule, c. 1966. The combined paybox and sales kiosk is quite attractive and was probably installed in the early 1950s. Cinemas were not yet in the business of making their own popcorn but sales of sweets, chocolate and ice-cream were becoming increasingly important in the struggle to make ends meet.

The Hillsborough Park Cinema, May 1966. On offer is a Norman Wisdom double bill of *The Square Peg* and *The Bulldog Breed*. The handsome brick building is faced with white faience, mainly above and flanking the entrances; the parapet is also covered in faience. The cinema opened on 10 February 1921. The hall was sited on filled-in ground and signs of instability developed, even before the building had been completed. While no serious problems developed, cracks in the back wall needed to be pointed up from time to time. The seating capacity of the cinema was about 1,300, including 400 in the balcony. There was a café and lounge at balcony level, which came to be used regularly in the evenings for solo and whist drives. In 1923 it was opened as a ballroom but within a year or so the card players were being welcomed back, although dances continued to be held occasionally. In April 1930 the hall went over to sound, British Acoustic equipment being installed. In 1931 the cinema was elaborately redecorated; the lounge was still used for dancing but mainly at private receptions.

Matinées were customarily held on Mondays and Thursdays but these were discontinued in 1952. Saturday morning children's matinées were announced in August 1955 but they were continued for less than two years. Sunday opening was given a trial in 1956 but it lasted for only a few weeks. The Park closed briefly for 'modernization' after being taken over by Star Cinemas in February 1960. Saturday children's matinées were restored and, while only advertised briefly in the press, probably continued until 1966. Sunday opening was also brought back and continued until the Park closed on Sunday 29 October 1967. It reopened ten days later for 'Star bingo'.

The Hillsborough Kinema House, Proctor Place, February 1965. The title of the film displayed on the illuminated sign is *Crooks in Clover*. The Kinema opened on or about 18 November 1912. Information on the building is scanty but sketch plans suggest a seating capacity of 850, of which 150 were in the balcony. By 1913 a 'day and night' screen was installed that gave a brighter picture. In 1920 the hall was closed for extensive alterations, including a new balcony; seating capacity was increased to around 1,150. The aim was to move the Kinema up-market. In the mid-twenties the Kinema was again re-seated, while the lighting system was altered; new automatic screen curtains were installed. In 1931 some reseating was carried out together with an extensive scheme of redecoration. In 1935 the appearance of the main entrance was enhanced by applying white faience cladding to the front wall, making changes in the paybox area and extending the proscenium frame. On the first night of the Sheffield Blitz in December 1940 an exploding landmine caused extensive damage to the roof and the Kinema did not reopen until October 1941. The new manager was (Walter) Clifford Wells, who had graduated from the position of chief projectionist; Wells continued at the Kinema until his sudden death in 1965. The Kinema did not open on a Sunday until May 1953 but Sunday programmes continued until the hall closed; they were different from those shown during the remainder of the week. The Kinema survived four years longer than the Walkley Palladium, the final programme being on 23 July 1966.

Five

Woodseats and Heeley Cinemas

The Heeley Electric Palace opened in August 1911 and was the largest cinema yet built in Sheffield; the Woodseats Palace followed in early September. These were the earliest purpose-designed cinemas outside the city centre with the important exception of the Hillsborough Phoenix. The Heeley Coliseum opened in October 1913 and was the last in the district to be built before the war. The Heeley Green Picture House opened in April 1920 and the Chantrey, which was appreciably larger, in May 1920. There had been no pioneering attempts to emulate such halls as the Hillsborough Palace of Varieties or the Walkley Electric Palace but the cluster of cinemas in Woodseats and Heeley were not dissimilar to those in Hillsborough and Walkley. The close association between the Walkley Palladium and the Hillsborough Kinema was matched by the link between the Woodseats and Heeley Palaces following the creation of Heeley and Amalgamated Cinemas in 1920. More striking, however is the similarity of roles played by the Hillsborough Phoenix and the Heeley Green Picture House. Whereas the Phoenix was given the title of theatre with the intention of incorporating variety turns in film programmes, the hall at Heeley Green only showed films until the later 1920s. While the Phoenix was a variety and revue theatre from 1925 to 1933, Heeley Green, now a theatre, operated in similar style from 1929 to April 1938. However, once films had returned both halls dropped the booking of live acts. Finally, a coincidence perhaps, but in 1935 improvements were carried out at both the Heeley Coliseum and the Hillsborough Kinema with a view to giving their main entrances a more distinctive appearance. Unlike the Hillsborough Kinema, the Woodseats and Heeley halls largely escaped damage from enemy action during the Second World War.

Chesterfield Road, looking towards the city centre, c. 1914. The Woodseats Palace is readily identifiable but the general scene is probably of greater interest.

Above: The Woodseats Palace, Chesterfield Road. The frontage of glazed terracotta was green and white and incorporated two small shops. The shape was unusual with domed turrets on the flanks. There was a side passage leading to a pit entrance. When it opened on 4 September 1911, seating capacity was only 550; the cheap seats at the front were on tip-up benches. There was a small stage and three dressing rooms but no curtains; the screen was lifted up when there were occasional variety turns. There was only a single kineto-projector; access was through the manager's office and up a perpendicular ladder. In 1920 a balcony was constructed, the projection booth being moved downstairs; seating capacity was increased to around 800. From 1923 to 1946 the manager was Byron Peach, who came as projectionist when the Palace opened. In early 1955 the hall was acquired by Star Cinemas; it closed for a fortnight for 'modernization' and work necessary prior to showing films in Cinemascope. The Palace for the first time opened on a Sunday, while children's Saturday matinées were given a new lease of life. However, it closed on 24 September 1961.

The Chantrey Picture House, Chesterfield Road, 1922. It had opened on 22 May 1920. There were a series of ornamental brick arches along the Chesterfield Road frontage, while terracotta had been extensively used on the façade above the entrance. Its capacity was about 1,400, including the balcony seats. At the time there was considerable interest in the 'Clavorchester', which was played as a musical background to silent films and also was featured in solo performances. It was devised by Charles Brindley of the Sheffield organ builders; a similar instrument was later installed at the Abbeydale Picture House and the Victory Palace. It had become fashionable to provide tea rooms in cinemas, while another potential asset was a ballroom. It appears to have proved less successful than had been hoped and eventually dancing gave way to billiards. The first sound film was the popular *Sunnyside Up*, which was shown in April 1930. In the following year an improvement scheme involved refurnishing, redecoration and new lighting, while the hall closed for a week in 1938 for refurbishment and the installation of the latest sound equipment. A panoramic screen preceded the introduction of Cinemascope in February 1955. The hall closed on 28 February 1959, a date which was the manager's sixty-fifth birthday; William Brown had come to the Chantrey in 1948 and had previously been manager at the Forum. The Chantrey had never opened on a Sunday. The building was reconstructed to provide offices for Gleesons, the contractor who had been involved when the cinema was built.

Below opposite: The Palace confectionery kiosk as remembered by Peter Bolt and recreated in his Woodseats home, May 2001. The aged onlooker was reminded of the brand names of the sweets he bought as a child. The exhibits date from the turn of the century to the 1950s.

Left: The Heeley Green Picture House, Gleadless Road, February 1959. The cinema opened on Easter Monday, 5 April 1920. It was quite an attractive building in mock Tudor style. Seating capacity was around 980 including the balcony. Variety turns were first included in programmes towards the end of 1926. In 1927 various improvements were made including the installation of a fireproof curtain, while in 1928 the stage was enlarged. After a period of transition, the picture house was used as a theatre from April 1929 staging variety and revues; however, in the summer of 1930 the hall reverted briefly to films while the dressing room facilities were being improved. In 1938 the proscenium was reconstructed and other work undertaken with a view to the hall being relaunched as a cinema, which opened on 9 May. Its fortunes were very similar to other suburban cinemas and audiences fell away in the 1950s. It closed on 7 March 1959 but reopened under new management as the Tudor on 3 April 1961. Despite many attractive programmes it did not prove possible to turn back the clock. According to the register of cinematograph licences the Tudor closed on 14 July 1962, although the last press advertisement was six weeks earlier.

Right: The projection booth, Heeley Green Picture House. Gaumont projectors were installed in 1938 coupled with British Acoustic 'Duosonic' sound equipment. The chief projectionist was Jack Potter, who later became the cinema manager. In 1949 GB-Kalee projectors and sound equipment was installed.

HEELEY PICTURE PALACE. SHEFFIELD.

The Heeley Palace, London Road, at the junction with Oak Street, possibly *c*. 1912. The cinema opened on 7 August 1911 as the Heeley Electric Palace, the frontage being coated in white cement stucco. Seating capacity was 1,450 including 350 in the balcony. There were three boxes on each side of the auditorium, while in 1913 five additional boxes were provided. Despite the trappings of a theatre, it was never the intention to include variety turns. In 1915 there was a demonstration of Kinemacolor, a pioneer process requiring a special projector. In 1917 an organ was installed, constructed by the Sheffield firm of Brindley and Foster. One of the problems was that the orchestral pit was liable to flooding and eventually it became necessary to protect the console by placing it in a steel tank, which was an obstacle the organist had to climb over every time he performed. Frederick Holmes, who had been Jasper Redfern's manager at the Central Hall, was appointed manager at the Palace in 1914 and remained until 1937. In 1950 the hall was closed for three weeks for 'modernization', which included re-seating and the installation of the latest 'Westrex' sound equipment. When Star Cinemas took over in 1955 Sunday opening was introduced, while children's matinées were regularly held on Saturdays. However, by the early sixties the company was already considering the disposal of the site to property developers. The Palace first closed as a cinema in March 1963, although children's matinées continued. After a period as a bingo hall, it reopened as a cinema in February 1965 but with a number of bingo sessions. By this time the hall had become rather dingy and there were no screen curtains and it finally closed as a cinema on 22 June 1965.

Heeley Coliseum, London Road, at the junction with Guernsey Road, January 1961. Built on a rather restricted site, it opened on 27 October 1913. It was one of many cinemas of the period where the frontage was surfaced with white faience. A balcony is referred to in 1922 and was probably incorporated in the original building. Seating was reported at the time of opening as 600 but it was probably slightly higher. The First World War brought prosperity to the cinema trade but it was not sustained in the industrial slump that followed. Because of a fire in adjacent premises it had become possible to acquire a little extra land and it was intended to provide a more attractive and prominent entrance from London Road and increase seating capacity. However, it seems unlikely that any major work was possible until the mid-thirties. The advertising image remained 'the little theatre with the big pictures'. The hall did not go over to sound until August 1931; of cinemas within the city only the Page Hall was later. In 1935 the Coliseum was closed for two months and reopened in October following partial demolition and rebuilding. The old pit entrance was converted to a balcony foyer; also at balcony level there was now a large waiting room. There was an increase of over 100 seats in the balcony, made possible by the removal and repositioning of the projection booth, while there was also increased seating in the stalls, bringing the overall capacity to 900. A primrose-coloured front of vitrolite glass with black and green enrichments imparted a more contemporary appearance. The entrance doors were of glass with chromium-plated fittings; a canopy was erected a few months later, while in 1939 a new proscenium was constructed. A panoramic screen was installed in 1955, films being shown in Cinemascope from May 1956. The hall closed on 14 January 1961. It had never opened on Sundays.

Six

Cinemas Serving the Housing Estates

The Manor Cinema was the first and was particularly well sited on Manor Top. It opened in December 1927 but the Paragon, which would become the equivalent hall serving the Firth Park area, did not open until October 1934. It was another three years or so before the Ritz was in business at Parson Cross and the Plaza at Handsworth. By now the boom in cinema construction was well under way. In August 1938 the Carlton opened on the Arbourthorne estate, soon to be followed by the massive Forum on Herries Road. The Rex at Intake opened in July 1939, probably looking to attract audiences from a wider area. Lastly was the Capitol, which was about to open when the Second Word War, perhaps fortunately, brought a halt to a time when each suburb hoped to have their own cinema.

The derelict Carlton remained an eyesore for many years but was eventually demolished. Unfortunately no photograph has been traced of what it looked like when in full flow as a cinema. It opened on 15 August 1938. The building was unusual in being constructed throughout in concrete but in the top half the concrete incorporated brick fragments, the surface being bush hammered to impart a slight gloss. Despite the austere appearance, the interior was quite attractive, the decorative features being accentuated by a system of coloured lighting. The auditorium walls were partly covered with wood and plaster to improve the acoustics. Seating capacity was 1,222 of which 351 seats were in the balcony. The first and only manager was Arnold Burrows, who remained throughout the war and post-war years. It closed on 7 February 1959. The cinema was never open on Sundays for entertainment purposes, although prior to the war it had been used for Sunday religious services.

The Rex cinema at night, highlighting the balcony foyer and café; Rex is signed in red neon.

The Rex cinema, Mansfield Road, at the junction with Hollybank Road, October 1981. Designed by Hadfield and Cawkwell, it opened on 24 July 1939. The exterior was mainly faced with rustic bricks, which contrasted with the blue tiles of the tower; blue tiles were also used around the entrance. An important feature was a full-length cantilever canopy, above which was a long horizontal window to the balcony foyer. The frontage included two shops, one of which was retained for the sale of sweets and chocolates; a hatch connected with the entrance hall for the convenience of those patronizing the cinema. A fragment of news attracted interest in 1944, when customers wearing clogs were warned that they would be refused admission because of damage caused to carpets and fittings; iron-shod clogs were particularly damaging. The Rex was regarded as a family house and films rating an X certificate were seldom booked. The first feature to be shown in Cinemascope was *Rose Marie* in March 1955. From 1958 Saturday afternoon children's matinées became a regular event. From 1970 the cinema closed for some two or three days before Christmas and sometimes for the whole of Christmas week. The Rex was destined to become the last surviving suburban cinema in Sheffield, It never became involved in bingo; nor did it open on Sunday until September 1981, when it had been leased to Northern Cinema Services, a Leeds based firm. Despite the initial hopes the venture did not prove a success and the Rex closed on 23 December 1982 with a double bill of *Chariots of Fire* and *Gregory's Girl*.

The Rex entrance hall, August 1939. The staircase leads to the balcony foyer. To the right of the paybox (but not shown in the photograph) were a number of broad steps leading down to the stalls foyer. Details of possible interest are the tiled floor and the wall mirror. The display board beneath the paybox shows the film title, performance time and British Board of Film Censors' certificate. The films being advertised are only half visible but were *Dangerous Medicine* and from Thursday *Garden of the Moon*.

The Rex balcony foyer and café. There is a long upholstered settee for patrons waiting for a feature to end before going into the auditorium. The tables and chairs are of tubular metal construction. During daylight hours the window on the left would provide ample natural lighting and possibly quite an interesting view for those who have ordered tea and something to eat.

The Rex auditorium. Those were the days when all cinemas had screen curtains, often attractively lit. The original seating capacity was 1,353 of which 342 were in the balcony but by the mid-seventies capacity was down to just under 1,000.

The Rex projection booth. Super Simplex projectors were replaced in 1967 by BTH mark 2 projectors. The projectors shown appear to be Kalee 21s, while the original Peerless magnarc lamps have been converted to xenons. The use of T and R rectifiers suggests that the photograph was taken in the mid-1970s or later. Although two projectors are still required, the spools are larger than those previously in use and would run some thirty minutes before a changeover was necessary.

The Forum, Herries Road, opposite the junction with Herries Drive, June 1955. With a seating capacity of 1,814, the cinema was the largest on any of the housing estates. It opened on 17 September 1938. The red-brick building was on a steel frame, the main circle girder weighing thirty tons. White faience was used to highlight the façade and also the fin tower, which bore the name of the cinema in red tubular lighting. The walls of the auditorium converged on the screen and were perforated by ventilation vents; the screen curtains included one of festooned satin, which looked most attractive in a blend of coloured lighting; there was also a stage safety curtain. Lawrence Cellini, the first manager, had something of a flair for publicity. One of his idiosyncrasies was to include jokes in his press advertisements which, although unrelated to the film, doubtless caught the reader's eye. From October 1942 to May 1943 the Forum was promoted as a cinema that offered films, music and variety. A new giant ampliphonic organ was launched, which was played during the ensuing weeks by a number of visiting organists. Between one and three turns were presented, sometimes in a double-feature programme. In 1942-43 there were a series of Sunday charity concerts. The Chairman and main shareholder of Forum Cinema (Sheffield) Ltd had been Michael Gleeson but Essoldo acquired a major stake in the company in November 1947. The hall first opened on a Sunday in February 1948. The Forum was equipped to show films in Cinemascope with the enhancement of stereophonic sound, although not until April 1955. It was eventually renamed the Essoldo, Southey Green, in June 1956. From December 1961 the hall introduced bingo for one evening session a week but film programmes returned in May 1962. However, from November 1967 the cinema remained closed on Wednesdays and the final performance was on 31 May 1969.

The Paragon, Sicey Avenue, between North Quadrant and Stubbin Lane, July 1950. The cinema opened on 1 October 1934 and was the first to be built in Sheffield since the coming of sound. The architects were Hadfield and Cawkwell, who were later associated with the Ritz and the Rex. The construction was of sand-faced bricks on a steel frame, the cinema frontage including two shops. The canopy, main doors and half round pillars at the entrance were faced with stainless steel. The entrance vestibule gave access to a lounge, which served as a waiting space, and at balcony level there was a lounge and café with tubular steel furniture. Seating capacity was 1,386, including 352 in the balcony. The seating incorporated vermilion, beige and black, providing a colour motif which, with variations, appeared in various parts of the house. The proscenium opening of 40ft was unusually wide; it was flanked by black and gold pillars. The side curtains and pelmets were vermilion and the main curtains beige; silver festooned screen curtains were chosen and colourfully lit. Simplex projectors had been installed, adapted for the RCA Photophone High Fidelity sound system; in the later forties these were replaced by Ross projectors. Matinée performances were soon dropped in the thirties but regular matinées on Mondays and Thursdays were held from 1941 to 1956, although there was a gap in the early fifties. In 1939 a covered queue shelter had been constructed that ran the full length of the building on the North Quadrant side. The Paragon was a hall that was seemingly ideal for the installation of a wide screen and Cinemascope was presented from February 1955, the first feature being *The High and the Mighty*. The cinema closed on 28 February 1962; it had never opened on Sundays.

The Manor Cinema, September 1956. The outside of the building was of rustic brick with wide bands of coloured cement dressings. The hall was on a steeply sloping site and the circle, sometimes referred to as the first balcony, was on the level of the entrance hall. From here staircases led up to a second balcony and down to the saloon, which was at parterre level. The cinema opened on 12 December 1927 with a seating capacity of 1,680. A billiard hall in the basement was completed in April 1928. Projection was from the rear of the upper balcony: the screen was hung in front of a curtain that covered the whole of the back of the stage. A combination of coloured lights could be thrown on to the curtains and continuously changed. The hall went over to sound in April 1930. In 1936 a canopy was erected over the entrance. In 1950 a modern-style proscenium was introduced, which was imaginatively decorated and lighted. In 1955 the projection suite, which had previously been at the upper balcony level, was relocated at the back of the saloon. In July 1956 the cinema again closed, the work including the extension of the proscenium to 35ft; the hall reopened with its first presentation in Cinemascope. In October 1958, following acquisition by Star Cinemas, further improvements were carried out including the installation of new sound equipment. In celebration there was a firework display featuring 120 rockets, one for each cinema in the Star circuit. No time was lost in publicizing Saturday children's matinées at 10 a.m. and 2 p.m., while Sunday opening followed almost immediately. The Manor first closed as a cinema on 21 July 1963 but within a few days was operating as a bingo hall, although children's matinées were still held. However, on 17 November 1963 the Manor was back in business as a cinema, although some bingo sessions were retained. Final closure was not until 14 June 1969.

The Ritz at the junction of Wordsworth Avenue and Southey Green, February 1938. It opened on 6 December 1937. The exterior was mainly of rustic brick but featured a series of vertical concrete ribs holding glass bricks; through these natural lights reached the balcony and staircases. The sides of the auditorium tapered towards the proscenium, which at 47ft was exceptionally wide; it was flanked by heavy red curtains, while the screen was covered by a golden curtain on which a varied array of lights was thrown. Seating capacity was 1,673 including 440 in the balcony. RCA Phototone sound equipment was installed with BTH projectors. The first manager was William McDonald, who was the younger son of the chairman, but he was serving in the Forces in the Second World War; at the Ritz, Bernard Dore held the fort from November 1940 to October 1944, Stanley Cunningham taking over until McDonald's return.

Although there was a sizeable stage, there was neither wing nor fly space; nor were there dressing rooms. During the war years there were occasional charity concerts on Sundays; the stage also proved useful for improvised entertainment at children's matinées. The first presentation in Cinemascope was in June 1955. McDonald left to manage the Tudor in April 1961, the Ritz having been acquired by Star Cinemas. The hall closed in July for 'modernization', which included contemporary style décor, new carpeting, improved seating and the installation of new projection equipment and lighting. Saturday children's matinées were relaunched, while a bingo session was introduced on Sunday evenings. However, apart from children's matinées, which continued, the Ritz closed as a cinema on 7 November 1962. After operating as a bingo club for $2\frac{1}{2}$ years, films were again shown from 17 May 1965. Films were shown on Monday, Tuesday, Wednesday and Saturday evenings, while bingo continued on Sunday, Thursday and Friday evenings. The Ritz finally closed as a cinema on 9 November 1966. It must have been one of the few Star cinemas that had never shown films on a Sunday.

Bernard Dore and staff at the Ritz, c. 1943. Bernard Dore was born in 1900, being brought up in West Bar, a part of Sheffield then noted for its music halls. He was a choirboy at St Vincent's church and took pride in turning the projector handle at film shows in the church hall. Later he got to know the projectionist at the Don Picture Palace and learned the ropes as a rewind boy. He was eventually accepted in the Forces and after the war was able to organize film shows for the troops. Demobbed in 1920, he landed on his feet as chief projectionist at the newly opened Wicker Picture Palace. As a projectionist he later worked at the Electric and Globe cinemas in Barnsley. His first job as manager was in 1939 at the Regal, Doncaster, but towards the end of 1940 the opportunity arose of going to the Ritz when the manager left to go into the Forces. The Ritz was a fine new cinema and he remained four years. Mindful that the previous manager would have the right of reinstatement on demobilization, Bernard took the plunge and in October 1944 joined forces with Star Cinemas, initially at the Lyric; by the end of the European war he was also working at the Stocksbridge Palace, preparatory to taking over as manager. It was at Stocksbridge, in particular, that he made his mark but in 1954 he decided to return to the familiar surroundings of the Don Picture Palace, where he had been offered the post of manager. After about seventeen months he returned to Stocksbridge, although the spectre of bingo proved a thorny problem. Shortly before it closed as a cinema, he was transferred to the Hillsborough Park, which was one of Star Cinemas' more recent acquisitions. Dore carried on as manager when it went over to bingo but retired in April 1973. He continued on a part time basis as relief manager at the Abbeydale and Studios 5, 6 and 7. Bernard Dore was always interested in cinema history and was the Sheffield Cinema Society's first President. He died in September 1996 at the age of ninety-six.

The former Ritz in 1988, as a bingo hall. The Ritz was one of the cinemas designed by the local architects, Hadfield and Cawkwell. Kenneth Friese-Greene's Sheffield-based firm specialized in theatrical work and was heavily involved in providing the furnishings. As a bingo hall, the Ritz proved a great survivor, but has recently closed.

The former Capitol/Essoldo/Vogue in 1988, still looking in fine fettle as a bingo hall. To correct a fallacy, an organ was never installed at the Capitol, although it had occasionally been visited by touring organists, performing on their own electric organs.

The Capitol, Barnsley Road, close to the junction with Deerlands Avenue, October 1939. After the Forum this was the second cinema in which Michael Gleeson was both proprietor and building contractor. Gleeson had again used George Coles, a nationally recognized cinema architect. It opened on 18 September 1939, shortly after the outbreak of war. Coloured brick was relieved by cream faience, which was also used on a fin projecting at one end of the façade. Seating capacity was 1,716 of which 500 were in the balcony. The proscenium width was 36ft. There was quite a large stage and four dressing rooms. Within ten days of opening, variety acts had been introduced on Friday nights as an added attraction. However, the big names were to appear in a series of Sunday charity concerts, mainly staged between November 1942 and September 1945. Among the entertainers were Tommy Handley, Vic Oliver, Rob Wilton, Turner Layton, Tessa O'Shea, Cyril Fletcher, Ronald Chesney, Sonnie Hale, George Formby and Rawicz and Landauer. The Essoldo circuit controlled Gleeson's cinemas from November 1947, although the Capitol was not renamed the Essoldo, Lane Top, until April 1950. The first Sunday opening was in February 1948 on the same day as the Forum. In 1953 *The House of Wax* and other films were shown in 3D. The first feature in Cinemascope was programmed in June 1954; it was the third cinema in Sheffield to show films in Scope and the second equipped to screen prints with a stereophonic sound track. Harry Telford Brown opened the Capitol and remained manager until 1956, although he had also acted as the Midland Circuit Controller for Essoldo. In April 1972 Essoldo sold its surviving halls to Classic Cinemas, who now operated the former Capitol as the Vogue. This was a name used by the company to avoid confusions when there was already a Classic established in the locality. The Vogue closed on 4 October 1975, having remained open three months longer than the Abbeydale.

The Plaza, Handsworth, at the junction of Richmond Road, Bramley Lane and Bramley Drive, February 1938. The cinema had opened on 27 December 1937. The building was faced in rustic brick, although the tower was surfaced in faience. The entrance on a corner site was dominated by a long sweeping canopy. There was ample waiting space in the entrance hall and foyer: stairs led on either side to the balcony. Total seating was just over 1,100. The auditorium was decorated in fibrous plasterwork; the colour scheme was orange for the flank walls, paling to a light buff at the ceiling. Around the base of the walls was a dado of Royal blue. Illumination was provided by concealed lighting in troughs in the ceiling. The extractor for the air conditioning installation was in the upper part of the elevational tower. The projection booth was equipped with a Western Electric 'mirrophonic' sound system and Kalee No. 11 rear shutter projectors, illuminated by Regal arc lamps. There were only two managers, the first being George Turner, who was succeeded in December 1957 by Colin Arnold. The hall closed for redecoration and refurnishing in July 1947. The cinema opened on Sundays from May 1953, while children's Saturday matinées were introduced from April 1954. The first feature in Cinemascope was *Three Coins in the Fountain*, which played in March 1955 with the enhancement of stereophonic sound. In September 1962 the cinema closed for redecoration. In 1962 and early 1963 a number of musical groups and variety acts were booked as one night stands, which were not combined with a film programme. In 1963 the hall was acquired by Kerner Entertainments Ltd and it closed as a cinema on 29 September 1963.

Seven

Some of the Other District Cinemas

The Upperthorpe Picture Palace had opened in December 1909 and the Roscoe Palace twelve months later but these were makeshift premises that would eventually be replaced. The Crookes Palace was a purpose-designed cinema that opened in November 1912, while the Unity Palace followed in November 1913 and the Oxford Palace in December 1913, although this was a reconstructed chapel. The opening date of the Weston Palace is uncertain but it would have been in mid or late February 1914. The Greystones Palace opened in July 1914 and the Rutland Palace around the beginning of February 1915. Of the post-war cinemas the Page Hall opened in May 1920 and the Abbeydale Picture House in December 1920. These were followed by the Scala in December 1921, the New Roscoe in April 1922 and the Sunbeam Pictures in December 1922.

In a history that is embroidered around a compilation of photographs it is hardly possible to give a full account of any individual cinema. The aim has been to convey some basic information and then select points of detail that hopefully may prove of interest. Taken together, an overall picture may be gained of many of the features of cinemas of the period when they were built and trends that developed through changes in practices within the film industry, some of which were due to technological progress. The most far reaching of these was the coming of sound for once the paying public decided what it wanted, it would not be denied. In Sheffield and elsewhere the wave of sound installations fell mainly within a period of twelve months from June 1929. Hallamshire Cinemas moved more cautiously and the halls with which it was associated did not convert until May or June 1931. These were the Crookes, Weston, Lansdowne and Darnall Picture Palaces. The last of the Sheffield cinemas to go over to sound was the Page Hall in November 1931.

An artist's sketch of the Abbeydale Picture House, in which every detail is carefully recorded; the ballroom entrance is shown at the side of the cinema.

Abbeydale Picture House, May 1970. The handsome brick building was faced with white faience on the extensive frontage visible from Abbeydale Road. It opened on 20 December 1920. Among the features were a series of Ionic pilasters and swags around circular windows, while a domed tower was skirted by a balustrade. An unusual feature was a fly-tower, which provided for the possibility of using the hall as a theatre. On each side of the proscenium there were two Ionic pilasters and, above the screen, was a panel of Grecian figures, which were obscured in 1954 when a large panoramic screen was installed. Above the box office vestibule was a lounge and café foyer for waiting patrons. The projection booth was at the rear of the balcony, while the rewind room was in the dome. In addition to an orchestra of some ten musicians, a 'Clavorchester' was installed in 1921; this was a two manual orchestral organ, made in Sheffield by Brindley and Foster. Harold Coombs remained a popular performer on the organ from 1922 until he left in 1933. Various improvements were made in the autumn of 1928, including the enlargement of the stage and upgrading of dressing room facilities with a view to introducing cine-variety; however, variety was discontinued with the arrival of talking pictures in April 1930. Some fifteen years later Cinemascope was ushered in with *Seven Brides for Seven Brothers* in April 1955. During the previous month the Abbeydale had been acquired by Star Cinemas and the new management lost no time in pursuing its twin goals of Sunday opening and Saturday children's matinées. The Abbeydale survived far longer than most suburban cinemas, although the stalls were closed from October 1974. The final programme was on 5 July 1975.

The Abbeydale auditorium, but the dating is uncertain. It had been extensively redecorated in August 1949, when matinée performances had been suspended. The walls are elaborately decorated both at stalls and balcony level. The curved ceiling is also panelled by decorative ribs and moulded pattern. In 1920 twelve workmen had been injured while decorating the auditorium; this had occurred when scaffolding collapsed. There is also uncertainty regarding the seating capacity, although in 1934 it was 1,560.

The capacious ballroom opened in September 1921. It remained a popular venue for dancing, particularly during the years of the Second World War.

The former Abbeydale building when occupied by A. & F. Drake, *c.* 1988. The premises were converted for use as an office furniture showroom and warehouse, although care was taken to retain many of the hall's distinctive features. The former cinema was subsequently 'listed' Grade II as being of architectural and historic importance. In 1991 Drake ceased trading and the building remains largely unused, although there is a bar and a basement snooker hall.

A poster shows the Rutland programme, for a week in July 1939. *Hell's Angels* was a 1930 film of aerial combat, re-released in 1939 in a heavily cut version. In the second half of the week, *Reckless Ranger* was an above average Western.

Neepsend Lane in June 1939, with a rather distant Rutland Picture House at the junction with Burton Road. The hall had a stone frontage but the most noticeable feature was a beacon-like domed tower. There was a covered passage from Burton Street providing shelter for those in the queue. The opening date was probably on or about 1 February 1915. From the outset there was a balcony and seating appears to have been around 760. Interior decoration was in red and cream. There was a stage and two dressing rooms but little, if any, use seems to have been made of these facilities. The projection booth and rewind room were at ground level and there were two Kalee projectors. In 1922 J.H. Greenfield, one of the projectionists, claimed to have invented a flickerless shutter and arranged with a manufacturer to market the instrument. In July 1926 the hall was closed briefly for redecoration. In April 1931 it was refurnished and again redecorated but various improvements were made. In particular, seating capacity was increased to 900 and British Thomson-Houston (BTH) sound equipment installed. In 1934 further decoration was carried out, on this occasion through Kenneth Friese-Greene's Sheffield-based firm.

Kenneth was less well known than his father, William Friese-Greene, but was financially more successful. His firm, which from 1941 traded as Modernisation Ltd, provided a useful service to those operating cinemas and theatres. Once problems were identified, detailed schemes of improvement were put forward and work agreed was undertaken at a fixed negotiated price. The Rutland rarely advertised in the press until the Autumn of 1940. The hall was damaged on the first night of the Blitz and never reopened. *Hitler, Beast of Berlin* had been showing earlier in the week. A sign advertising the film survived long after the cinema had been put out of action but without the last two words of the title.

Unity Picture Palace, Langsett Road, between Gertrude Street and Wood Street, 1921. It was opened on 7 November 1913 by Upperthorpe Picture Palace (Sheffield) Ltd, which had previously pioneered the Upperthorpe Picture Palace, a small hall in Cross Addy Street. The building was mainly brick with imitation stone dressings. The façade to Langsett Road consisted of an arched entrance and a series of five bays divided by broad pilasters having moulded capitals supporting a stone frieze; this had 'UNITY' carved at intervals. Seating capacity was 990 including the balcony, where the seats were of the tip-up variety and upholstered in velvet; seats in the pit were more Spartan and entered from Gertrude Street. The curved ceiling in the auditorium was divided into a series of panels by enriched plaster beams. At the level of the springing of the ceiling was a cornice, broken at intervals by blocks, from which hung moulded pendants of fruit, flowers and leaves. There was a small stage and dressing rooms; some variety acts were booked in the spring of 1914 but the trial was not regarded as particularly successful. The first manager was Harry Bramwell, who had moved across from the Upperthorpe Palace: he remained at the Unity until he died in 1934. Another manager who was highly respected by his colleagues was Frank Neal, who came in 1940 and stayed until his retirement in 1956. The Unity succeeded in business without really trying to catch the headlines, although it was one of the Sheffield cinemas that exploited Cinemascope by showing it with stereophonic enhancement. It closed on 28 March 1959, never having opened on Sundays.

Oxford Picture Palace, junction of Addy Street and Shipton Lane, May 1962. Opening on 15 December 1913, the converted building incorporated much of the original structure of a Unitarian chapel; the altar remained intact behind the cinema screen. The architects were Hickton and Farmer, who were also responsible for the Electra and the Cinema House. The frontage was covered with white stucco; there were decorative leaded-light windows, including a large arched window above the front entrance. Tapestries were displayed in the entrance lounge, while there were tapestry panels on the walls of the auditorium, fibrous plaster work on the ceiling and, surmounting the screen, figures representing music and literature. There was a balcony with a total seating capacity of possibly 900. The Oxford was one of the halls that became part of Heeley and Amalgamated Cinemas in 1920. Christopher Ramsay, who had been manager for ten years at the Alexandra Theatre, came to the Oxford when it closed in 1914 and remained until he transferred to the Attercliffe Pavilion in 1933. Ramsay died on 10 December 1940. Two days later the Oxford suffered minor damage in the Sheffield Blitz but it appears to have reopened by Christmas. Star Cinemas took over from Heeley and Amalgamated in January 1955, installing a much larger screen in readiness for the showing of films in Cinemascope. Although matinées had been held for a number of years on Mondays and Thursdays, children's matinées were now held on Saturdays, both in the morning and afternoon, while the Oxford opened for the first time on Sundays. In 1960 the cinema was hired on Sunday afternoons by an ethnic minority group so that members might see films in their own language. The Oxford survived longer than many suburban halls but closed on 15 August 1964 with an admirable double bill, which would have pleased Peter Sellars fans, of *Two-way Stretch* and *I'm all right Jack*.

The former Roscoe Picture Palace, at the junction of Jobson Road with Infirmary Road, in 1990 during its days as a bingo emporium. The New Roscoe, as it was then called, opened on 17 April 1922. It replaced the original Roscoe, which was a converted works. It had opened on 23 December 1910 as the People's Electric Palace but within a few weeks the cinema was known as the Roscoe. It had been intended to build a new cinema shortly after the end of the war but an unforeseen difficulty arose when the city council used its emergency powers and placed an embargo on non-essential buildings. However, work started in November 1921 on a site alongside the old building, which would have remained open until mid-January 1922. The seating capacity of the new hall was about 900, including the balcony. The main entrance was at the proscenium end of the hall. The first manager was William Dodson Twigg, who left in 1924 but returned in 1936, remaining in post until his death in the early 1950s. The cinema went over to 'talkies' in October 1930, choosing 'symplaphone', a system that was not installed elsewhere in Sheffield; in 1938 it was replaced with a British Thomson-Houston (BTH) sound installation. In 1931 an extensive scheme of reseating and redecoration was carried out through Friese-Greene's firm; the work was completed within ten days without interfering with the normal running of the cinema. A novel feature was a Japanese rockery garden in front of the proscenium in a position once occupied by the orchestra. The first Sunday performance was in November 1952. In July 1953 a wide curved screen was installed. Cinemascope was presented with stereophonic sound but not until September 1955; this involved the removal of some front seats. Saturday bingo was introduced a few weeks before the cinema closed on 23 September 1961. The hall was leased to Kenneth Kerner and reopened within a fortnight as a cinema with bingo sessions on Wednesday evenings. However, it finally closed as a cinema on 22 April 1962, bingo then taking over.

The Crookes Picture Palace, at the junction of Crookes with Nerwent Lane. The film title below *Hit Parade* may possibly be *Magnificent Obsession*, which was shown in November 1955. The Palace opened on 2 November 1912, its name being embossed on a decorated cement façade above the entrance. Those queuing for admission lined up in an alley that ran alongside the hall. The architect was Walter G. Buck and the general contractor Joseph Enoch; both were directors of Crookes Picture Palace Ltd, a situation that was not uncommon. There was a raised section at the back of the auditorium, somewhat misleadingly described as a balcony. The decoration was in white and subdued crimson with the seats upholstered in red. Seating capacity was probably about 800. There was a Pathé projector. Music was provided by a Tyler cinfonium, an instrument that could produce a range of sounds imitating piano, harp, zither, violin, banjo, flute and guitar. Later a trio took over. The first 'talkie' was shown in June 1931, Western Electric equipment being installed. The first film in Cinemascope was *My Sister Eileen*, which was shown in June 1956. Sunday performances had begun in June 1955, while children's Saturday matinées were held from December 1955 to December 1959; for a time both morning and afternoon matinées were fitted in. The Crookes Palace survived three years longer than its sister hall, the Weston Picture Palace, but closed on 2 April 1960.

The former Greystones Picture Palace, now a bingo hall, 1982. Before the end of the year the premises were to be destroyed by fire. It opened on 27 July 1914, the brick building being faced with stone dressings on the Ecclesall Road frontage. The architect was J.P. Earle. The walls of the auditorium were cream with an Indian red dado; draperies were in a deep crimson colour. There were some 700 seats, tip-up throughout, but only in the balcony and rear part of the saloon were they covered in velvet plush. There was a small stage and changing facilities. From October 1914 a basement ballroom was available with an attached kitchen. There were two Powers projectors. Substantial alterations were completed in July 1920, seating being increased by around 120; there was a new café lounge and the ballroom had been extended. William Rogers, one of the directors, was persuaded to take over in 1925, when the manager left unexpectedly, and was retained in that capacity until his accidental death in 1942. In 1930 additions were made to the projection booth and BTH sound equipment installed. The first 'talkie' was *Sunnyside Up*, which was shown in April 1930. About the same time the ballroom was given a maple sprung floor. A car park was completed early in 1936. William Bradley was appointed manager in the early forties but he died in 1953; his wife Ethel was able to take on the duties of manager until the cinema closed.

A panoramic screen was installed, the first film in Scope being shown in July 1955. There was a fire in August 1956. The cinema was out of action for five weeks but the greater damage was to the ballroom. Some work was carried out in 1957 under a Friese-Greene contract, most probably involving redecoration. In August 1962 the cinema closed for three weeks while various repairs were carried out and a new ballroom floor laid. The cinema had never opened on a Sunday and closed on 17 August 1968. The auditorium was reopened as a bingo hall, while the ballroom eventually became a nightclub.

The former Page Hall Cinema, Idsworth Road, around 1995, when in use as a carpet depot and snooker hall. The mainly brick building was on a sloping site. A series of pilasters was intercepted by a wide cemented band that was separated from an ornamental roof parapet by a series of circular windows. The cinema opened on 24 May 1920. There was a balcony, total seating capacity being about 1,300. There was an orchestra of some eight musicians. The café was not opened until August 1920 but became a popular venue for whist drives. There was also a billiards room with space for eight full-sized tables, but this was not ready until February 1921. In 1929 a ballroom was added; situated behind the screen, it had a separate entrance. The Page Hall Cinema did not go over to sound until November 1931; it was the last Sheffield cinema to do so. In 1945 the cinema was acquired by the Buxton Theatres Circuit and renamed the Roxy in November 1945. For nearly six months in 1946 matinées were suspended to facilitate a programme of reseating and other renovations. However, in November 1946 the hall came under the management of Reiss (Cinemas) Ltd. Jack Reiss was actively involved in running the cinema, although commuting from Leeds, but there was a resident manager. Sunday shows were first held in January 1946 but were discontinued in October, most probably because of the impending change of ownership; they were resumed in February 1947. A fire broke out in January 1958, probably originating beneath the screen platform. The cinema was quite badly damaged: a new screen that had been installed two months earlier was destroyed, as was part of the balcony. The ballroom was undamaged and remained in use. The cinema did not reopen until June 1958, when *The Bridge on the River Kwai* was shown; despite the late date, this appears to have been the first feature shown in Cinemascope. The Roxy probably closed on 14 June 1959, the cinema reopening as a bingo hall, while the ballroom became a dancing school.

The Sunbeam Pictures on Barnsley Road at the junction with Skinnerthorpe Road, June 1961. This handsome brick and stucco building, set back from the road, opened on 23 December 1922. The architect was Walter G. Buck, who was also a director of the company that owned the cinema. There was an ornamental parapet that incorporated an embossed rising sun motif. The Sunbeam was one of the cinemas delayed as a result of the city council's decision in 1920 to ban non-essential building so that labour and materials would not be diverted from housing. The seating capacity was variously stated but 1,350 was probably around the mark; there was a balcony. Seating was described as luxurious with tub divan tip-ups and ample leg room. Within a few weeks of opening prices were reduced, bringing them into line with East End halls. In 1927 a billiards hall was opened adjoining the cinema. The Sunbeam went over to sound in January 1930, which was earlier than most district cinemas. Unfortunately the system chosen, 'Cinephone', was only suitable for films where the sound had been recorded on disc; it was replaced in January 1932 with Western Electric equipment following a decision by the production companies to standardize on optical sound. In 1935 a shelter was completed at the side of the cinema, while the following year the canopy over the entrance was extended. The hall first opened on Sunday in September 1954. The first Scope feature was *A Star is Born*, shown in April 1956. The cinema closed on 2 September 1961, after giving the kids a last treat with *Son of Sinbad* and *Tarzan's Hidden Jungle*.

The Woodhouse Picture Palace, Market Place, c. 1925. The building in brick and embossed concrete incorporated two small shops. An unusual feature was an external balcony projecting over the front entrance. The auditorium included a small balcony with a total seating capacity of some 600. The cinema opened on 2 March 1914, performances being twice nightly with a children's matinée on Saturday afternoon. Later a Wednesday morning matinée was introduced for miners on shift work. After a few months variety artists appeared on the bill fairly regularly but only until the summer of 1916. In December 1919 the hall was bought by a company that was planning to build the Scala. In August 1920 the Palace closed so that the balcony could be carried forward several yards; this increased its seating capacity from 100 to 220. The hall was refurbished and two new Simplex projectors were installed. By the time it had reopened at the beginning of December, Woodhouse had become part of Sheffield as a result of a boundary extension. Until 1942 there remained a separate entrance to the pit, access being to the left of the main entrance and along a passage at the side of the cinema. Balcony seats could be booked but only on a Saturday night and bank holidays. A crucial appointment was made in 1926 when Harold Booth became manager; he remained at the hall until it closed in 1957, a period of thirty-two years. The hall went over to sound in November 1930; in order to accommodate the bulky sound equipment, it had been necessary to extend the projection booth above the external balcony. In 1937 the cinema was briefly closed for refurbishment and the opportunity was taken to reset the speakers to improve the fidelity of sound reproduction. The installation of a wide screen involved structural alterations to the stage, the first film in Cinemascope being shown in July 1955. The Palace never showed films on a Sunday; it closed on 28 December 1957.

The former Scala, Brookhill, at the junction with Winter Street (now closed), 1963. The Arts Tower is rising in the background. The Scala opened on 23 December 1921. The brick and terracotta building was in the style of an Italian opera house. There were basement assembly rooms, where whist drives were often held in the 1920s. The café was at balcony level; from 1942 to 1949 it was used as a municipal restaurant. The ballroom was at second-storey level, although it did not open until October 1922. By 1928 the interest in silent films was noticeably flagging and for some ten weeks a singer, musician or variety artist was engaged in the hope that attendances might improve. The popularity of sound films proved a more successful remedy. *The Broadway Melody* came to the Scala in October 1929. It was only the fifth Sheffield cinema to go over to sound. Effie Swindin, who was daughter of the Scala chairman, was appointed manager in early 1930 and remained in the post until the cinema's premature closure in 1952. Business improved to such an extent that for a long period in the 1930s matinées were held every afternoon except Fridays. In 1936 a Friese-Greene contract involved the construction of a new proscenium front and a scheme of redecoration and refurnishing in matching colours. Richard Ward's *In Memory of Sheffield's Cinemas* draws attention to a strange coincidence. The *Sheffield Telegraph* reported an air-raid precaution exercise on 13 December 1938 with the headlines 'City cinema hit in air raid' and 'Scala bombed'. Exactly two years later it actually happened on the night of 12/13 December 1940. The Scala's roof was severely damaged and the cinema did not reopen until 7 July 1941. The future of the Scala was blighted by Sheffield University's planned expansion and the cinema closed on 5 July 1952. However, it was over ten years before the University was able to start building and, in the meanwhile, the Scala building was used by the Department of Biochemistry. It was finally demolished in 1964.

The Scala auditorium, 1923. The balcony curved round the auditorium, which was decorated with polished grey wood and mahogany panels. Total capacity was 1,020 of which 400 seats were in the balcony. The screen was at the same end of the building as the main entrance.

The Scala entrance hall, 1923, which was embellished with panels of grey birchwood relieved by a pink marble dado and pilasters. On entering, the paybox was on the right; a short flight of steps led to the saloon, while there were staircases on both sides leading to the balcony, the one on the right also serving as an approach to the café and ballroom.

The film unit at Sheffield University is run by the students for the students. Since 1949 it has provided film shows in a variety of venues but mainly at Graves Hall in the students' union building at Western Bank. In 1972 Graves Hall was reconstructed to provide better viewing conditions. However, by 1996 the hall was required for other purposes.

In the meantime the University had built a purpose-designed auditorium of the stadium type, equipped with a Cinemeccanica Victoria 5 projector and a CNR-35 Platter. The original Dolby processor has been upgraded so that audiences may enjoy the latest in quality sound reproduction. The seating is as comfortable as it looks.

Eight
Multiplex Cinemas

The age of the multiplex dawned in Sheffield when AMC opened a ten-screen multiplex at Crystal Peaks in May 1988. A multiplex has been defined as a cinema complex with five or more auditoria but it is probably a mistake to tie down the concept to a given number. The twinning of the Gaumont in 1968/69 signalled the end of the one cinema, one screen era, as did the opening of Cinecenta with twin auditoria in 1969. It is difficult to enthuse over the makeshift Cineplex, which was derived from three shop units, while ABC 2 in 1975 and Gaumont 3 in 1979 were small auditoria created by hiving off space previously used as a café or restaurant. The building of a purpose-designed multiplex offered the best chance of providing attractive conditions for film viewing, capacity being geared to market expectations. However, the Odeon off Arundel Gate was a conversion of a multi-storey building incorporating the Cinecenta auditoria and the disused Fiesta night club. By the time it opened in March 1992, UCI had taken over the multiplex at Crystal Peaks. Warner (now Warner Village) Cinemas opened a multiplex at Meadowhall in March 1993, while Virgin followed with a mammoth twenty-screen multiplex at the Valley Centertainment Leisure Park; this opened in November 1998 and is currently operated by UGC. While some may regret the loss of cinemas such as the Gaumont and the ABC (later Cannon), the multiplex offers the opportunity for one-stop shopping, while the range of auditoria of varying sizes is better suited to present-day audience levels. The films shown are mainly recent releases, the more successful running for weeks or even months. The Showroom is in a category on its own, exhibiting a greater proportion of foreign or other minority interest films. However, UGC is currently testing the market by showing a number of so-called 'art-house' movies in its smaller auditoria. The people of Sheffield are indeed fortunate in having a wide choice of both cinemas and films but it is never wise to take good fortune for granted. 'Use it or lose it' is an adage that can be remembered too late.

The Virgin Megaplex by night, January 1999. When UGC took over from Virgin in November 1999, the logo and trademark was replaced by a UGC motif.

The café bar in the Virgin Megaplex, November 1998. Here seen from the upper level approach to the auditoria, the café bar is situated on a mezzanine level. During daylight hours there is ample natural lighting. The décor provides a restrained but slightly unconventional setting, enhanced by strip lighting on the escalators and chrome-plated handrails on the stairway. Virgin Cinemas (now UGC Cinemas) are adjacent to the Valley Centertainment tram station and opened on 5 November 1998. Constructed of coloured blocks on a blue-brick base, extensive use is made of white-coated metal panels, while the ventilation louvres are of coated aluminium. A central glass façade extends to the parapet level and carried the Virgin logo. The ground-floor layout has recently been modified with the relocation of the box office stations. There are twenty auditoria. Originally designated as 'Premier Screens', auditoria 19 and 20 offer an intimate and luxurious setting; they are situated just off and to the right of the vestibule. The remaining auditoria at ground level are accessed along the corridors leading from the back of the vestibule: auditoria 1 to 7 are to the left and 8 to 11 to the right. There are similar corridors on an upper level reached by escalator or lift; there is also a central stairway. Auditoria 6, 7 and 12-15 are to the left and 7, 8 and 16-18 are to the right. There are two entrances to 7, the largest of the auditoria; there are also entrances to 6, 7 and 8 at ground level. The auditoria are quite steeply tiered. Total seating is 4,915, the capacity of the auditoria ranging from 82 to 691; additionally, there are at least two wheelchair places in each auditorium. The screens are slightly curved and range in width from 23ft to a gigantic 61ft. There are no screen curtains and no masking. There are two projection booths at a lower and one at an upper level, where a series of connecting channels gives access to widely dispersed projectors. Kineton FP40 projectors have been installed throughout with 'Tower' units and platter systems. Sound encoded on Dolby Digital may be reproduced in all auditoria, while auditoria 6, 7, 12, 19 and 20 have the option of utilizing DTS (Digital Theatre Systems) in which sound is recorded on compact discs. Auditorium 7 is also equipped to handle SDDS (Sony Dynamic Digital Sound), a facility not available at other Sheffield cinemas.

The Warner Village multiplex, May 2001. From February 1997, most Warner Cinemas have been rebranded following an agreement with Village Roadshow, another exhibitor with a worldwide cinema network.

Warner Cinemas, Meadowhall, opened on 23 March 1993, the entrance being from the first floor concourse of The Oasis. Within the entrance and on the left was a shop trading in sweets, ice-cream and popcorn; to the right was a computerized box office. However, the entrance became very congested at peak periods and at the end of 1994 the box office was relocated on an island site some 25 yards away; the shop was also moved and is adjacent to but not within the entrance. The cinema complex is constructed on three levels with a fourth projection level. From the entrance foyer an escalator leads to a lower vestibule at ground floor level; there is also a winding staircase for those leaving after the show. The lower vestibule contains a prominent concessions stand. Throughout the building the dominant colour motif is yellow and blue. Access to auditoria 4, 5 and 6 is on the right of the vestibule, while further along there is a corridor leading to auditoria 1, 2 and 3. From the entrance foyer a short flight of steps leads to a corresponding upper vestibule giving access to auditoria 7 to 11. The auditoria differ in both size and design. In the larger auditoria all but the first few rows are steeply tiered, while in others the floor is only slightly raked. Traditional screen curtains have been retained. Current seating capacity is 2,198, the auditoria ranging from 95 to 358 seats; in addition there are 36 wheelchair places. There are two projection booths with portholes at both sides. These are at levels two and four, servicing respectively auditoria 1 to 6 and 7 to 11. Christie xenon consoles and platter systems service ten Simplex and one Century projector head. 70mm projection is possible in the largest auditorium. Dolby sound is currently installed in all auditoria and in 5, 6, 7, 8, 10 and 11 it has been upgraded to SRD (Spectral Recording Digital); DTS (Digital Theatre Systems) is also available in nine of the auditoria.

The Showroom, April 1998. The display panels are advertising Martin Scorsese's *Kundun* and (below) the Norwegian *Junk Mail*. The Showroom was formerly a garage and motor repair depot on a site bounded by Paternoster Row and Leadmill Road, which is at an appreciably lower level. The cinema opened on 2 March 1995 but with only two auditoria. A bar and café were added in April 1997 and, with the aid of substantial lottery funding, the Showroom reopened with four auditoria on 27 March 1998. In the final phase of the development a new main entrance had been constructed off Sheaf Square. There is a small lobby with a door on the right leading to the bar, while the entrance to the cinema vestibule and box office is on the left. All seats are numbered and may be booked in advance. The original auditoria (Cinemas 1 and 2) are at the upper ground level, as are the café and Showroom 5, a multipurpose education and conference space. Cinemas 3 and 4 are on the lower ground level, a spacious lobby giving access to the main toilets. Seating capacity is 83 in Cinema 1; 110 in 2; 178 in 3 and 280 in 4 – a total of 651. In Cinema 3 there is a block of seats, accessed from aisles on both sides, while in Cinema 4 there is a central aisle, with the back rows being steeply tiered. There is a single projection booth for Cinemas 1 and 2 with 35mm Provost projectors; there is also a 16mm portable Fumeo machine. Provost projectors also serve Cinemas 3 and 4, where there are separate projection booths. All projectors are fitted with xenon lamps and a platter system is in operation, although in Cinema 3 two projectors are available to revert to a changeover system, which is a requirement when handling archive prints. Cinemas 1 and 2 are equipped to show Dolby SR (Spectral Recording) prints, while in Cinemas 3 and 4 the equipment can exploit the advantages of Dolby Digital prints; the option of DTS (Digital Theatre Systems) is also available.

The Multiplex was renamed UCI on 11 August 1989. It had opened as the AMC (American Multi-Cinema), Crystal Peaks 10 on 26 May 1988, the cinema complex being regarded by the developer as an anchor unit within the shopping centre. However, AMC decided to pull out of the UK market, its cinemas passing to UCI (United Cinemas International), a joint venture between MCA (Universal) and Paramount Pictures. There is a single computerized box office with four terminals and collection points for telephone bookings made by credit card. The box office is flanked by doors leading to a large reception area. An illuminated sign indicates the films being shown, while details of the classification and performance times are displayed on smaller boards within the box office. Around the lobby, video screens transmit scenes from films currently being shown or coming soon. A fast food counter serves a range of snacks, ice-cream and soft drinks. The floor is tiled green in the vicinity of the counter and stone coloured elsewhere; however, the central area is carpeted. Toilet facilities are positioned on both sides of the lobby. There are two carpeted corridors arranged symmetrically leading to the auditoria, which are all on ground level: screens 1 to 5 are on the left and 6 to 10 on the right-hand side. Seating capacities range from 200 to 312 and the total is 2,328; in addition there are 30 wheelchair places. Background lighting is provided by thin strips of light attached to the edge of alternate wall panels, while there are tivoli lights along the edges of the aisles. There are five projection booths, each containing two Victoria 5 projectors. All auditoria have the capacity to play films in Dolby SR (Spectral Recording). The equipment in auditoria 3 and 4 has been upgraded to take advantage of Dolby Digital prints, while auditoria 5, 6 and 8 are able to utilize DTS (Digital Theatre Systems). Throughout the complex there are no screen curtains. Among the innovations has been the introduction of 'Directors' Chair' presentations on Tuesday evenings to cater for a more discriminating audience.

The Odeon, Arundel Gate, July 1999. In May 1999 there was a move to rebrand the Odeon image and the tiled exterior around each entrance was covered by stainless steel cladding. Overall the effect is impressive, particularly at night when the sign is picked out with fluorescent blue light. Odeon 7 opened on 5 March 1992. Of the seven auditoria, five were fitted into the shell of the former Fiesta night club, the remaining two being the original Cinecenta auditoria. Development was on three levels. At the top was a newly constructed entrance off Arundel Gate. However, the main entrance and box office was at an intermediate level, which was that of a subway then running under Arundel Gate. In the reception area beyond the box office there are opportunities to buy a range of refreshments, confectionery and snacks, while in the evenings there is access to a segregated bar area. Those coming into the cinema through the Arundel Gate entrance need to walk down a flight of steps but there is also a second stairway leading up to screens 1, 2 and 3 past a mural depicting nineteenth-century Attercliffe. Screens 4 and 5 are off a corridor beyond the reception area but at the same level. Those making their way to screens 6 and 7 need to continue down a stairway to the lowest level. Odeon 7 dropped the 7 in December 1994 with the opening of screens 8 and 9; screen 10 followed but not until December 1997. These additional auditoria were accommodated in space vacated by tenants on the upper concourse of the multi-storey development. Capacities in the various auditoria range from 115 to 253 and with the opening of screen 10 total capacity rose to 1,714; there was also a total of 20 wheelchair places. There are screen curtains in all auditoria. There is a projection booth for each auditorium, the projectors being mostly Cinemeccanica Victoria 8s but the Philips FP 20s installed in the Cinecenta auditoria were retained. A 16mm Fumeo projector is also available at screen 5, an additional porthole having been provided.

Nine

The Fringe Cinemas

There were a number of cinemas in fringe areas of Derbyshire and the West Riding that are now part of Sheffield. Beighton became part of Sheffield in 1967 and Chapeltown, High Greem, Ecclesfield and Stocksbridge in 1974. By then the cinemas had closed, although most of the buildings were still in use. The first of these cinemas was the Electric Theatre in Stocksbridge, which opened on 18 September 1911. The Public Hall in Edward Street had been converted for use as a cinema with a raked floor and a fire-proof 'Bioscope box'. There were two projectors that were cranked by hand, although a generator provided electricity for illumination. The so-called circle seats were the back half-dozen rows of the stalls, which were the best in the house and very comfortable; the pit seats were wooden forms. The manager was Jack Haines, who was also the projectionist; he gained his early experience of 'animated pictures' as a travelling showman touring the fairgrounds. His wife was on the pay box before the show and then went to assist her husband in the projection box. There was a pianist but no usherettes.

The Chapeltown Palace opened in December 1912, the Central Hall, Beighton in August 1913 and the High Green Palace in January 1914. The Ecclesfield Cinema House opened in 1921 on New Year's Day, while the Stocksbridge Palace followed in May 1921. Everyone in Stocksbridge flocked to sample the delights of a new purpose-designed cinema but after six months or so people began returning to the 'old pictures'. The proprietors of the Palace reacted by buying out the opposition and promptly closing the Electric Theatre, the last performance being on 22 February 1922.

The Central Hall, Beighton, c. 1923. Following an extensive fire in 1922, the opportunity was taken to enlarge the vestibule by building single-storey extensions on both sides. There were now two entrances in place of the original central entrance.

The Central Hall, High Street, Beighton, c. 1934. The hall opened on 7 August 1913, the proprietor being Edwin Whiteley. Seating capacity was about 450 but some of it was on unpadded wooden benches. The cinema was gutted by fire on 29 March 1922 and did not reopen until September. In the auditorium the back few rows were now tiered and termed a balcony. The stage and dressing rooms had been retained and turns were booked from time to time. Occasionally there was a concert party or an evening of variety in place of films. Sandy Powell, Harry Korris and Elsie Carlisle were among the artists who appeared. Edwin Whiteley had taken over as manager with the help of his younger son, Edward, who was one of the projectionists. Edwin had lost his wife but later married Mabel Pettifer, a widow who was a pianist at the cinema. In January 1932 Edwin Whiteley died suddenly and Mabel took over as proprietor. Jack Pettifer, a son by her first marriage, became manager at Beighton in 1934. In August 1938 the Central closed for over two months. The hall was extended, the roof being raised at the screen end of the auditorium to accommodate the larger beam resulting from a longer throw. Seating capacity was increased to just under 600. The original central entrance was restored and shelter was now provided by a small canopy, while the brickwork was covered with cement rendering. Cinemascope arrived in August 1956 after the installation of a larger screen. By now there were three changes of programme weekly. However, in May 1956 the Central closed for a week after being sold to Star Cinemas. The hall was re-seated and the external lighting made more attractive. For the first time the cinema opened on a Sunday, while a children's matinée club was established on Saturdays. Bingo was introduced in August 1961 but for only a few weeks. However, the Central closed as a cinema on 23 March 1963 but was soon to emerge as the Central Casino.

The Central Hall, Beighton, *c.* 1938. The picture must have been taken before August of that year, when work was started on a major scheme to extend the hall. The films on the billboard are *Splinters in the Air* with the Yorkshire comedian Sidney Howard and, in the second half of the week, Frank Capra's *Lost Horizon* based on the James Hilton novel of a Tibetan Utopia.

The Chapeltown Palace, May 1913. It hardly looks like the same cinema as that pictured overleaf, but the two photographs were taken within a week of each other. *A Tale of Two Cities* was the 1911 version.

Chapeltown Picture Palace, Station Road, May 1913. The building was of brick with a Moorish-style exterior and white stucco front. The architects were Benton and Roberts, who were also responsible for the Sheffield Picture Palace. It opened on 23 December 1912. The seating capacity was approaching 700 and, while all seats were of the tip-up variety, those in the pit were not upholstered. The projection booth was outside the main hall at the level of the flat roof; there was an 'Indomitable' projector. The large stage came to be mainly used by the Chapeltown Amateur Operatic Society, who hired the hall for a week each autumn from 1925 to 1930. British Thomson-Houston (BTH) sound equipment was installed in January 1931. Plans to provide a balcony never came to fruition. In 1938 the hall was closed for a fortnight for re-laying the floor and installing new seating. This was re-spaced with a considerable loss of capacity. In March 1944 the Palace was taken over by Star Cinemas, programmes being changed three times weekly. Alfred Dawson, the chief projectionist, retired in 1954 after working the cinema since the day it opened. Films were first shown in Cinemascope in April 1955. The hall did not open on Sundays until June 1956. Bingo was tried out on Friday evenings from February to August 1962 but the showing of films was then resumed. The cinema closed on Saturday 16 March 1963. The Chapeltown Star Juniors' Club kept going to the end and even on the last day there were matinée performances at both 10 a.m. and 2 p.m. Three days later the hall reopened as the Palace Casino with Star Bingo.

The former High Green Picture Palace, Thompson Hill, in use as a warehouse, 1993. The hall opened on 29 January 1914, seating capacity being reported as 500. Frank Woffenden was both proprietor and manager for some twelve years. In 1929 the hall appears to have been leased to Arthur Dunn and his two partners. Some renovation and redecoration was carried out and it was announced that there would be double feature programmes and variety turns. In February 1930 the St John Ambulance Brigade were allowed free use of the cinema on a Sunday when a film was shown in aid of local funds. It was a full house and Mr Dunn was prosecuted for allowing people to sit on forms, which were considered to have obstructed the gangway and side exits. Western Electric sound equipment was installed in 1930 but no further details have been discovered. In April 1931 Woffenden again took over the reins with a view to selling the cinema as a going concern and it was bought by High Green Cinemas, a Chesterfield-based company controlled by Louis Barnes. In 1934 the sound equipment was changed to British Thomson-Houston (BTH) but during the following year the hall remained closed for several months. It reopened in September 1935, F. Goodwin Viner being the lessee; he may also have been the manager. By this time seating capacity was down to 311. The hall advertised in the *Penistone, Stocksbridge and Hoyland Express* in 1925 but only for a few months; press advertisements were resumed in 1938 and thereafter appeared fairly regularly, although not necessarily every week. From 1939 onward three programmes were shown weekly, each playing for two days. In April of that year Ralph and Hilda Thomas took over as proprietors and remained with the cinema until it closed. However, Ralph became increasingly disabled and Hilda – initially the cashier – found herself bearing the greater share of responsibility, although in the later years a son assisted as projectionist. In 1956 the couple installed a much larger screen, the first film in Cinemascope being shown in February. The cinema closed on 5 October 1957; Ralph Thomas died in May 1958.

The Ecclesfield Cinema House, The Common, *c.* 1929. The films billed are *Wild Cat Hetty* and *Number 17*, which would be the silent version starring Leon M. Lion. The cinema opened on 1 January 1921. Built of brick, the frontage was extensively covered by a white cement finish; two shops flanked the entrance. At roof level the words 'cinema' and 'house' fronted a parapet, being separated by an arched façade incorporating '1920', the year of construction. The total seating capacity was 685, of which the balcony accommodated 200. There was a stage with a 21ft proscenium and cine-variety was tried out in 1926, initially on a Wednesday and Saturday. Programme information is scanty but in 1928 there was a complaint to the licensing authority when a touring revue company was engaged despite the limited dressing room facilities. The hall closed around February 1931 but was reopened in March 1932 after the installation of Morrison sound equipment. Michael J. Gleeson who was a founder director, was the knight who rode to the rescue when the company was in serious financial difficulties. In 1938 a film of special local interest was *Sunshine Ahead*, which turned the spotlight on the Ecclesfield harmonica band. Jack Hodge, who was chief projectionist, was appointed manager in 1940, although in the later stage of the war his wife took over as manageress: an innovation which Mr and Mrs Hodge introduced was a series of Sunday concerts in aid of charities supporting those in the Forces. In 1947 the cinema was included in a deal involving the sale of the Capitol and Forum to Essoldo. However, the Cinema House was not advertised as an Essoldo cinema until April 1949, nor renamed the Essoldo, Ecclesfield, until September 1950. Films in Cinemascope were shown from November 1955. The hall closed on 7 February 1959; it had never opened on Sundays.

The Stocksbridge Palace, Manchester Road, July 1965. There would have been three changes of programme weekly. Built of red toned bricks with stone facings, it opened on 12 May 1921. An interesting feature was a bay window set at a high level and embellished with an ornamental stone support. The main entrance was flanked by two side openings but these were quite narrow and later blocked off; there was a side entrance for the pit. Seating capacity was 1,000 of which 300 were in the balcony; tip up seats were provided throughout. At first there was a small orchestra but by 1923 this had dwindled to a pianist and sometimes a violinist; but for some eighteen months that pianist was Reginald Dixon, then in his teens. The parting came about as a result of Dixon's demands for a better piano and, although probably justified, some might have felt that he had hastened its downfall as a result of his enthusiasm for special effects. There was a spacious stage enclosed by massive columns; variety acts would be booked when business showed signs of flagging. Wilson, Keppel and Betty and possibly Ted Ray were among the artists engaged. Projection was originally at ground level but, shortly before the coming of sound, a new projection booth was constructed; it extended over the carriageway at the side of the cinema, being supported on stilts. The first sound film was *Let us be Gay*, which starred Marie Dressler and Norma Shearer; this was in August 1931. In April 1942 the Palace changed hands when it was taken over by Star Cinemas. Bernard Dore was manager from 1945 to 1954 and for a second spell from 1956 to 1966. Children's matinées had been held previously on Saturdays but Uncle Bernard, as he was popularly known, took a particular interest in this side of the business, which gave scope for his talents as magician and ventriloquist. Sunday opening came in January 1953, while Cinemascope made its bow in November 1955. Bingo arrived at the beginning of 1962 with a Tuesday evening session, shortly to be followed by a Sunday afternoon session, which did not interfere with the evening cinema performance. However, on 11 May 1963 films were abruptly withdrawn leading to angry demonstrations. Within a few weeks films were back and from August 1964 all bingo was discontinued. Despite the rearguard action of 1963, the end was not long delayed. Saturday children's matinées were dropped from August 1964 but the cinema did not close until 23 July 1966. No public announcement was made of the closing but the building was boarded up immediately the Saturday night audience had left; after the dust had settled it reopened as a bingo hall.

Hoarding in Exchange Street. The programmes advertised for the week beginning 29 September 1924 cover the Empire, the Hippodrome, the Park Palace, the Wicker and the Greystones Picture Palace.

Bibliography

Allen Eyles, *ABC: The First Name in Entertainment*, Cinema Theatre Association, 1993 (includes a description and photographs of the Sheffield ABC)

Allen Eyles, *Gaumont British Cinemas*, Cinema Theatre Association, 1996 (includes a description, photographs and programme information relating to the Regent/Gaumont in Barker's Pool)

Leslie Frost, *Seats in All Parts. Memories of the Lyceum, Sheffield Empire and Attercliffe Palace*, published by the author 1986 (revised 1989)

Geoff J. Mellor, *The Northern Music Hall*, Frank Graham, 1970 (in particular, chapter nine on the MacNaghten Vaudeville Circuit)

Geoff J. Mellor, *Picture Pioneers. The Story of the Northern Cinema*, Frank Graham, 1971

Geoff J. Mellor, *Movie Makers and Picture Palaces. A Century of Cinema in Yorkshire 1896-1996*. Bradford Libraries, 1996

Picture House, magazine of the Cinema Theatre Association, No. 21, 1996 (includes details of the publicity stunts devised by Reginald Rea during a period when he was manager of the Albert Hall)

Clifford H. Shaw and Stuart R. Smith, *The Early Years of Cinema in Sheffield: 1896-1911*, Sheffield Cinema Society, 1995

Clifford H. Shaw and Stuart R. Smith, *Sheffield Cinemas – Past and Present*, Sheffield Cinema Society, 1999

Clifford H. Shaw and Christopher S. Stacey, 'A Century of Cinema' in *Aspects of Sheffield 2* (pp. 182-200), edited by Melvyn Jones, Wharncliffe Publishing, 1999

Fred Turley, *Mighty Music of the Movies: The Cinema Organ in Sheffield and the Surrounding Area*, Sheaf Publishing, 1990.

Richard P. Ward, *In Memory of Sheffield's Cinemas*, Sheffield City Libraries, 1988

Newsletters of the Sheffield Cinema Society, 1987 to date (copies deposited in the Sheffield Local Studies Library, which also holds contact addresses for anyone wishing to know more about the various local societies).